W9-AHD-177

THE SHADOW THAT SCARES ME

By Dick Gregory

FROM THE BACK OF THE BUS

NIGGER

WHAT'S HAPPENING?

THE SHADOW THAT SCARES ME

THE SHADOW THAT SCARES ME

Dick Gregory

EDITED BY

JAMES R. MCGRAW

1968

Doubleday & Company, Inc., Garden City, New York

Portions of the material in the sermons and the introduction have appeared in different form in *The Realist*, *Renewal* and *Cavalier* magazines.

Library of Congress Catalog Card Number 68–10561

Printed in the United States of America
First Edition

This book is dedicated to Ed Davis, one of the greatest philosophers I know, a man who can solve America's problems, and most of all, a friend of mine.

I owe a special thanks to these true Americans whose friendship and association have stimulated my mind and supported my spirit and made this book possible:

My wife Lillian
and the kids

Jim McGraw
Art Steuer
Ruby Burrows
Mike Watley
Jean Williams
Orzelle Billingsley
Jack Tanner
Herbert Jubirt
Jim Sanders
Bob Orben
Dick Shelton
Bernie Kleinman
Ralph Mann
Marv Josephson
Joe Glaser

The thoughts expressed in these prophetic sermons were developed during those years of rapid change between 1962 and 1966. They grew out of deep involvement in the civil rights movement and predate the 1967 summer of violence.

CONTENTS

MEET THE TURKEY GENERAL

BY Rev. James R. McGraw

You are about to read a book of impious sermons by Dick Gregory. In the best tradition of evangelistic preaching, these words have been spoken where the action is. Dick Gregory's pulpit may be the all-Negro church in the South or the all-white northern suburban church or the steps of Chicago's city hall. He has been preaching prophetic words in the midst of social crisis since 1962, when *We Shall Overcome* expressed the hunger for freedom. He continues to preach justice and truth today, as the new mood of the social revolution in America, a mood which Gregory prophesied and interpreted, is expressed by the words "*Black Power*."

Dick Gregory! The very mention of the name conjures up a variety of opinions and emotions. He has been described in show business columns as "the Will Rogers of our time," but those who know satire best liken him to Mark Twain. Bayard Rustin has called him "the Miracle Man of the revolution," Snick kids call him "our leader," and disapproving Mississippi whites designate him as "that millionaire nigger." He is loved and hated, admired, and berated, often misunderstood, and occasionally honored with laurels praising his almost superhuman efforts in the struggle for human dignity. But whatever the response, his is a voice our society *must* hear.

There are those who have said Dick Gregory lives in "two worlds" (*Holiday*, December 1962). They mean, I take it, the world of performance and the world of reform. But such segmentation of his life is as unreal as saying the clergyman lives in the world of the pulpit and the world of daily action. Every man, clergy and laity alike, has a variety of daily functions. Hopefully, there are certain standards, values, and ideals which dominate all our doing. And so it is with Dick Gregory.

Wherever injustice is manifest, Dick Gregory will soon be there. In June, 1964, word came to him that three young civil rights workers—James Chaney, Andrew Goodman, and Mickey Shwerner—were announced missing in Mississippi. Gregory was in Moscow, Russia, on a peace mission. That same evening, he joined James Farmer, then national director of the Congress of Racial Equality, in Philadelphia, Mississippi, to investigate the incident. He will fly from San Francisco to Chicago, from Los Angeles to Louisiana, to speak at a rally or to lead a march. And he will be back the same evening for his nightclub performance.

No demonstration is too small, no demand upon his time or personal finances too great. He has marched with a handful of pickets in Greenwood, Mississippi, and he has joined thousands of marchers in Montgomery, Alabama. And all at his own expense. His participation in the struggle for human dignity has cost him over a million dollars in travel expenses and canceled bookings. Add to that his innumerable legal expenses and you have a commercial rendering of the high price of freedom.

Gregory is nonviolent. Therefore he is a pacifist. He simply does not believe in killing. Consequently, he is also a vegetarian. His opposition to violence has placed him in violent danger of losing his own life. During the revolt in Watts, Gregory was shot and felled while trying to bring calm to the community. Momentarily stunned, he picked himself up from the ground, walked over to the man who shot him, took away his gun, and quelled his further participation in street activity with the words, "All right, goddam it, brother. You shot me. There's a hundred cops across the street that are fixin' to wipe you all out. So get the hell out of here." Only when Gregory saw the crowd leave would he allow himself to be taken to the hospital for emergency treatment.

Christmas, 1964, was a time of special satisfaction for Dick Gregory. And that Christmas story best illustrates his current status as the Five-Star General in the battle for dignity among men.

A few days before Thanksgiving, Gregory was returning from his latest visit to the battleground of Mississippi. The "soldiers" asked him when he would return. "I'll be back for Christmas," he replied. Even MacArthur didn't set a *date*. But at that moment, without realizing it himself, General Gregory had created the idea of a Mississippi Airlift.

On the plane to New York, he figured on spending Christmas in Mississippi with his wife Lillian and the kids (Lil had spent the previous Christmas in an Atlanta jail while she was still carrying the twins) . . . then he thought they'd take a Christmas dinner to a needy family down there and eat with them . . . but why not take a turkey to as many families as possible?

By the time the plane landed, Dick Gregory was committed to sending twenty thousand turkeys down to Mississippi for Christmas Day.

As his itinerant preacher, occasional chauffeur, and admiring friend, I naturally became involved. Greg had asked me to plan to spend Christmas with him in Chicago with his family. Now I was informed we would be flying to Mississippi instead, as turkey watchers.

The task of financing and executing the project began immediately. Seated on a rumpled bed in his hotel suite, General Gregory, clad only in a uniform of jockey shorts, made his initial telephone contacts.

It happened to be the week of the much anticipated Clay-Liston return match in Boston. Gregory calculated that The Bear and The Mouth could both use a charitable identification to clean up their tarnished images. What better tarnish-remover than *Christmas for Mississippi?*

"Get Sonny on the phone," the General ordered his First Lieutenant, Art Steuer. In a short time Liston, comfortably located in Boston, was on the receiving end of the Gregory charm. "Hey, baby, how's it look? Workin' hard? I'm fixing to send twenty thousand turkeys to Mississippi for Christmas. Thought it sure would be wild if you and Cassius would buy ten thousand apiece from the gate of the fight."

For the next half-hour the General strained to explain such things as tax deduction, publicity value, etc., to the surprised and bewildered ex-champ. He came off the wire with a tentative okay.

Next, Cassius Clay. "I want to speak to Muhammad Ali in Boston," the ever coy, intuitive, and diplomatic Steuer requested of the long-distance operator. After ten minutes of proper Islamic greeting, Gregory explained the same proposal to one of Ali's chief aides, the champ not being immediately available. "Just a minute. The champ just came in," was either the announcement or warning from the voice in Boston. "He says it sounds great."

The relieved and elated Gregory promised to check out prices and get to Boston the next day with all details.

The next lucky person to receive the Gregory treatment was columnist Drew Pearson. If you follow Pearson's column faithfully, you've probably noticed a conversion. In June, 1964, he had very little good to say of Dick Gregory, Adam Clayton Powell, and the whole crowd from ACT (a civil rights organization of "grass roots" leaders throughout the country). One entire column was devoted to Gregory, an open letter inviting him *not* to appear in Mississippi.

Then Drew made the fatal mistake of going to Mississippi himself.

Suddenly, new thoughts began appearing in his column. One beautiful article related his experience of sharing sweet potato pie with a Mississippi sharecropper family. The time was ripe to bring Pearson into the project. "Get Drew Pearson," were my orders from the General. I found him between planes in Kansas City. In this rather precarious position, I am sure he was glad to receive a call.

Greg grabbed the phone, and was amazed to hear Pearson's voice saying, "Dick, I just wanted to tell you that you were right and I was so wrong." Bang! Drew Pearson was hit with the idea of twenty thousand turkeys for Mississippi.

In a matter of moments, Drew became co-chairman of a committee called "Christmas for Mississippi." Immediately the project became tax-exempt—taken under the wing of America's Conscience Fund, an established organization under the leadership of Pearson and Harry Truman.

Complications began to develop. The General and Art Steuer flew to Boston the next day to make arrangements with the two gladiators. Instead they found the management in a clinch that could not be broken. The turkey negotiators returned with suspicions of what the next day would bring. It brought front-page headlines. Seems that the World Heavyweight Champion had discovered a hernia "the size of a small lemon," which the examiners just happened to miss a few days before. The championship bout became an even bigger lemon.

Sonny Liston, when informed of the tragedy, responded, "It could have been worse—it could have been me." Quipped the General, "Now how you gonna identify with a cat's hernia?" But Christian sensitivity would demand that I share the ex-champ's relief when he discovered that, this time at least, he didn't have to twist a knee or dislocate a shoulder. The fight was canceled. And so, along with countless bookies, twenty thousand turkeys flew the coop.

Undaunted, the General decided on two other strategies: street donations in Chicago, and a big benefit show on the same front. A "really big shew" demands a really huge star. Next stop, swank Ninety-third Street and the dwelling of the star of the Broadway smash *Golden Boy*, Sammy Davis, Jr. Our party of three strategists—Gregory, Steuer, and myself—was ushered into the modern palatial surroundings, Sammy's front man having been assured we had an appointment. We were invited to sip Scotch until the star descended the center staircase, à la Copacabana. When Golden Boy made his spirited entrance, he seemed nervous. Why not? A visit from Dick Gregory could mean an invitation to battle for a cup of coffee in an Alabama truck stop.

The suspense was killing Sammy. "Dick, we all know that you are on the front line more than any of us in show business. We feel it, but we don't know what we can do. A group of us in New York got together the other night to try to think of ways we could be in the struggle more." A perfect invitation, but Gregory played it cool. "Well, Sammy, I'm in a better position to be on the front line than anyone else. I'm not an artist. Don't have to perfect an act. Just look at my lines five minutes before my show, and if the line doesn't stick in my mind, it wasn't any good anyway."

The pressure was still on. Finally the General let him off the hook. "Let me see you alone for a couple of minutes." Golden Boy was visibly relieved. He was already forty-five minutes overdue at the *Tonight* show where he was guest moderator for the evening. The General emerged from the private conference with a firm commitment from America's greatest one-man show to appear at the Arie Crown Theatre, McCormick Place, Chicago, on Sunday evening, December 20.

The General and I flew to Chicago to set some gears in motion for collecting donations and selling tickets. Alternating my uniform of a black suit and clerical collar with a Santa Claus outfit, I manned my battle station at 6 A.M., each day a different corner. I stood at the bus /elevated change area with gaily painted red and green barrels covered with chicken wire. In Salvation Army fashion, I begged for handouts.

Once, as Santa Claus, I was challenged by two boys—too old, really, to believe in me—"Hey, you ain't the real Santa! That hair's not real!"

"Of course it is," I snorted. "Feel it." Less certain, but still belligerent, they insisted my beard and hair were definitely not real. "Listen," I reminded them, "just because it's not nappy, doesn't mean it isn't real."

Two teen-age boys, typical wise guys, came up and started joking with Santa. After about fifteen minutes of this, it became a drag, and the more exciting diversion was to pull Santa's beard. I responded, "I'm jolly Santa while we're cool, but don't cross me, baby." With a mixture of wonder and awe, one kid said to the other as they walked away, "Santa knows something."

One kid came up, pulled my beard, and announced with obvious hostility, "That's for last year, buddy."

Other kids came up to Santa, and Santa hugged them, talked to them, listened to them, and his heart sank! I knew these kids, or, at least, their cousins in Brooklyn. And I knew the pattern I was falling into—I knew what was expected of me, and the lie I was telling. The chance of Santa Claus stopping by their house on Christmas Eve was nonexistent. Dick Gregory's famous line took on new meaning, "My kids don't believe in Santa Claus, 'cause they know darn good and well no white man would be in their neighborhood after midnight." And here was Santa —me—acting just like Whitey always acts, telling that sweet-sounding lie, being a part of that cruel system.

"Santa, I want G. I. Joe . . . Chatty Cathy . . . roller skates . . . a bike." What do I say? That Santa's a phony, a fraud, a myth, a traitor? Then, what am I doing out there anyway? "Be good, and everything will be all right on Christmas." But it won't, you lying white Santa Claus, and you know it. *I* said that, not the kids, because they don't fully know it yet. Even when Santa was trying to help, even when Santa knew what the system had done to Mommy and Daddy and would eventually do to the kids looking up at him with those big, expectant, and worst of all *trusting* eyes—even then he ends up telling the old familiar lies. And believe me, he is ashamed—ashamed of the system and ashamed of his part in it; ashamed of a social structure in which the supreme symbol of charity and pure giving is distorted to become an agent of disappointment, bitterness, and cruelty.

Santa Claus learned that he is the supreme symbol of the lie.

But there was real beauty in the thrilled little giggle of a girl in her late teens, as she dropped one dollar in the barrel and said, "I've never helped Mississippi before." There was real beauty in the sacrifice of a wino, who reached into his pocket and gave four pennies to help someone in Mississippi. You have to understand what four cents means to a wino to appreciate it. That puts him farther away from that half-pint. Who knows how long it will take to hustle up the needed change for that bottle? But he's helping his brother in Mississippi. As it had been painful to see the reactions of the kids to Santa, it was sheer beauty to see the reaction of the winos.

The day of the Big Show was upon us almost before we realized it. Charles Evers and Drew Pearson flew into Chicago. Charles, brother of slain civil rights leader Medgar Evers and state field secretary for the NAACP in Mississippi, had been in charge of setting up the distribution of turkeys at their final destination. Co-chairman Drew had been collecting donations from his many contacts in high places. Everyone assembled in the General's headquarters.

Drew Pearson, impressively arrayed in a black Russian-style hat and black top coat, sat down and began removing two-thousand-dollar, five-thousand-dollar, ten-thousand-dollar, and twenty-thousand-dollar checks from his coat pocket, as casually as if they had been telephone messages. The General briefed his staff on the number of tickets sold, the money needed to get the turkeys rolling to Mississippi, and the last-minute details which needed attention. Then he sent Drew and Charles to the Jack Eigen Show for an interview.

Back in New York, United Airlines had a limousine

at the stage door of the Majestic Theatre waiting to pick up Sammy, who rushed out the door, following his Saturday night performance, and raced to Kennedy Airport, where the last flight from New York to Chicago was being delayed until his arrival. It was red carpet all the way. Special matchbooks had been made with the inscription "Welcome, Golden Boy."

Everyone was nervous. Even the General, although he would never admit it. "Wear your collar tonight, Rev," he said. "When I call you up on the stage, I want them to see we have God on our side." About half the house had been sold up front, at the box office and elsewhere, at ten, twenty-five, and a hundred dollars per seat.

Other performers rallied to help in the benefit. Eartha Kitt was playing the Palmer House and agreed to perform. George Kirby was in town and let it be known that he would be proud to be on. Red Saunders' band was on the bill, and at Red's rehearsal in the afternoon, the Four Step Brothers showed up to volunteer.

At 7:30 P.M. we stood in the lobby of the Arie Crown Theatre and waited. Lil Gregory in her maternity clothes, and I in my piety clothes, were ready to hand out programs. The General was on all fronts at once, handing me tickets, picking up tickets, handing me money, notes, and tidbits of information to remember. His capacity to combine the function of usher, ticket agent, producer, and performer was amazing. Our nervous jitters were soon to be quelled. The good people of Chicago began pouring in.

The General followed the Step Brothers, having been introduced by co-chairman Pearson. "People say it's foolish to send all those turkeys to Mississippi, when the people don't have anything to cook them on. When the Ku Klux Klan hears what we're up to, they'll burn enough crosses to roast an elephant. Anyway, they can just break off a frozen wing and have a turksicle."

He introduced Eartha Kitt. And after her sultry performance he quipped, "Eartha sounds like good chitterlin's supposed to taste." George Kirby closed the first half of the show, with an Apollo Theatre-type performance of gags and impersonations.

The General had his own personal moment of pleasure. He read off a list of names, each of whom received a special reward, a plaque or trophy from the most magnificent display of trophy hardware ever assembled on stage. Each token of appreciation was inscribed: *World's Champion Turkey Raiser, "Christmas for Mississippi," Dec. 20, 1964, and First Prize Human Being. Thanks for being Tom Paine's "Wintertime Soldier"—Dick Gregory.**

The sensation, however, was the presentation of Sammy Davis' award—a trophy bigger than Sammy himself. The General presented it, saying, "There wouldn't be a single turkey in Mississippi this Christmas if it wasn't for Sammy." Golden Boy was almost speechless with surprise and emotion. He finally said, "In the words of the vernacular, This is somethin' else!"

Then the stage was cleared, and the most versatile entertainer in the history of show business held the audience spellbound for the next two hours and fifteen minutes. He sang, he quipped ("You know my biggest problem these days? Finding Kosher pigfoot." . . . "My mother was Puerto Rican, my father was colored, I converted to the Jewish faith and married a white woman. There aren't too many neighborhoods I can move into"), he did impersonations and played every instrument in the band. And when it was over, the audience seemed more exhausted

* See list of "Wintertime Soldiers" at end of book.

than Sammy. He could have done another show, but the rest of us were worn out.

And the General spent the next day in bed. The battle won, his rest was earned.

Wednesday, December 23, 1964, was T-Day. Two refrigerated trucks were already rolling from Iowa and one from Chicago. All of us turkey watchers gathered at Butler Field painfully early in the morning. Rather heavy fog choked the atmosphere, and we were somewhat dubious about the possibilities of getting off the ground. It was a crisp morning, and the well-wishers huddled in little circles chatting excitedly. A truck was being unloaded when we arrived, five hundred turkeys slowly ascending the conveyer belt into the awaiting cargo plane. The turkeys were joined by hundreds of toys and games, donated by toy manufacturers in Chicago.

The General boarded the cargo plane as chief turkey watcher; and Lil Gregory, two of their daughters—Michelle and Lynne—Ed Davis and myself boarded a Delta Airlines flight to Jackson, Mississippi. Ed Davis, the member of our party that made it an even half-dozen, is the street corner philosopher of Harlem's Seventh Avenue and 125th Street. Any Saturday evening, when the weather is at all cooperative, he can be seen atop his stepladder, raspily proclaiming his nitty gritty philosophy, with the aid of a beat-up hat and rubber-faced grimaces—a sort of black Frank Fontaine. His proclamation is definitely Black Nationalist oriented, and this trip was his first contact with this integration stuff. The General was hoping for a conversion.

Our planes landed simultaneously at the Jackson Air Terminal. The General descended from the plane, in uniform, looking (to quote AP) "splendid in buckskin boots, a three-quarter-length black leather jacket and a cowboy hat." The press was obviously friendly, for they could have had great fun with the fact that Dick was munching on a big, black cigar. He should have been chewing Redman, just to keep up the Mississippi image. An integrated crowd of over one hundred had been waiting two hours for our delayed arrival.

Surviving the onslaught of the gentlemen of the press, we were quickly engulfed by the Mississippian reception committee—Charles Evers, surrounded by benevolent Baptist preachers, civil rights workers, and bodyguards. Charles was all smiles. "Welcome to the Magnolia State, land of the brave niggers and home of the nervous white folks." As a truck backed up to the cargo plane to unload toys, and turkeys, we went first to Evers' home to get settled.

I sat on the sofa in Charles' living room. On the mantel were the pictures of two martyrs—Medgar Evers and Jack Kennedy. Between the pictures was a rifle. I thought nothing of this, other than that Charles was probably a hunter, until I looked in the corner next to me and saw a sawed-off shotgun. A quick glance about the room showed me a gun in every corner, which, I was later to discover, was the situation in every room. Outside the house was a twenty-four-hour-a-day armed guard.

"They'll probably get me," said Charles, "but not like they did Medgar, not in the back going into my own home."

From his home, we went to the Pratt Memorial Methodist Church, where the Jackson contingent of recipients were waiting to receive their Christmas dinners. The total impression upon arrival was that of Easter morning, without the usual concern for dress. Over eight hundred people were jammed into the sanctuary—standing room only and more and more arriving. Our crew of officiating preachers crowded behind the pulpit and began competing with one another to read off the names of the lucky winners. The resulting confusion was not unlike a traditional Sunday morning display.

The five hundred turkeys from the plane disappeared quickly, but another load of cargo was expected momentarily from Chicago. Heavy fog delayed the arrival, but the driver checked in to Jackson at all points of his route. And the people waited; waited with patience beyond the point of reasonable expectation. Some of them had been waiting all night long for that curious frozen oddity. This may sound strange, but at least 90 percent of the people had never had a turkey before.

Fanny Lou Hamer, of Freedom Democratic party fame, had told us of this. "I'm forty-seven years old, and I've had a turkey once in my life, and I had to buy it on the installment plan." And now we saw that it was true. We saw it in the faces of those who received the first five hundred. We saw it in the tears of pure joy and gratitude, streaming down worn and weary cheeks. This was the most beautiful sight I have ever seen.

A lady said to the General, "I got fifteen kids and I make fifteen dollars a week. I don't have to say no more . . . thanks." Another looked up and said, "Mawnin', Lawd." In the most pious voice he could muster up, the General intoned, "Yes?"

These people had only one thing to give on Christmas—honest and sincere gratitude. And now they were completing the joy of the act of giving, begun by their brothers and sisters in Chicago, by their act of pure and heartfelt gratitude.

That night a rally was held at the Masonic Hall on Lynch Street in Jackson.

In a protest move, the White Citizens Council of Ruleville, Mississippi, announced that they were sending two possums and a sack of sweet potatoes to Gregory in Chicago. "Sending me food," the General announced, "that's like sending a relief check to Rockefeller. They don't know my background: I'd jump over a whole carload of sirloin to get to a good possum. Why, I could sell those possums on the black market in Chicago and get enough money to send down two hundred more turkeys.

"*We* didn't raise this money and send these turkeys. *You* did. It's *your* fault. You have completely purged this state of negative thinking. It's easy to raise money for Mississippi, because of you. Everybody who eats anything this Christmas will think of you.

"We brought turkeys for the champs. You earned that. What you're doing in this state has put a lot of people off our backs.

"When you integrated that golf course down here, the cat in New York begins to wonder, 'Where's mine?' Same thing with schools and libraries.

"Some people up North said that Sammy Davis was scared to come to Mississippi. Well, he probably is! If the President of the United States hasn't been to Mississippi in fifty years, why should Sammy come? Well, if the President won't come to Mississippi, take it to him! Take your kids to the White House on Easter when they have the big egg roll on the lawn. Just dump your little ole kids on the lawn and say, 'We want to play too.'

"White Folks praise Bob Hope for going to Vietnam and criticize me for coming to Mississippi. Well, it's safer in Vietnam. At least there you know the government is on your side."

The next morning that truck from Chicago still hadn't arrived. The driver called about 9:30 A.M., and said he was in Columbus, Mississippi, and was on his way. All the second nighters were crowded about the candy store in front of the NAACP offices on Lynch Street. More tired, a little more weary, but no less patient, they waited expectantly. I talked to a man who came from a little community about fifty miles outside Jackson, Brookhaven.

"How long you been here?" I asked.

"Two nights and a day . . . that's as long as Christ was in the grave," he replied.

"Well, I guess you can look for some pretty big things to happen today," I suggested.

"Yeah. . . . I guess I better be lookin' for a raisin'."

About 2:30 P.M., the truck pulled in. The response of those patient bystanders was like that of the people lined along the streets in old World War II newsreels, when the liberating American troops pulled in, amidst cheers and looks of gratitude. I had seen such a response once before, when bus after bus rolled into Washington, D.C., the day of the "March for Jobs and Freedom." David Brinkley's camera crew was set up on Lynch Street. They had been told that if they didn't get some exclusive pictures, they shouldn't bother to come back to work.

The General, Evers, and I jumped on the back of the truck and began handing out turkeys. There was one white man standing far in the back of a large crowd of Negroes. Evers called to him, wishing to show clearly on national television that this was, indeed, an integrated project (in fact, fifteen hundred turkeys went to whites, three hundred to a reservation of Choctaw Indians, and a number to Chinese families). The white man protested violently, indicating that he had a "bad back." Suddenly, it dawned on me that the poor fella thought we were going to make him unload the truck! I shouted, "We just want to give you a turkey!" Full of white reassurance, he ran to receive, forgetting, evidently, about his bad back. Thus did Huntley and Brinkley get their exclusive, "The First Man to Receive a Turkey in Mississippi Was a White Man."

All kinds of motor vehicles were there to load up with turkeys and take them to the out-of-the-way districts. Farmers with their dilapidated flatbed trucks, and city dwellers with their station wagons. One woman suffered a heart attack, she was so excited. But when the ambulance arrived to take her away, she told the driver, "Don't take me to no hospital, I'm gonna cook this bird in the mawnin'." And she drove home in a car with friends.

The General describes the scene by comparing it to a breadline anywhere—"people waiting to be fed in China, in the Congo, in Vietnam, in Europe . . . they all have the same faces. As I watched them it dawned on me, this is man's *number one job;* before he lands on the moon or Mars, or cures another disease, or invents another invention, he has to feed man all over the world. . . ."

That night, we went to Gulfport. We checked on the distribution of turkeys there, and stayed at the twenty-million-dollar Broadview Motel, guests of the white lady owner. Evers and company had desegregated this particular public accommodation a few months before. Now she insisted that the General and his staff sleep there. We were given a luxurious three-room suite, two spacious double bedrooms, and a huge parlor. We had dinner in the dining room as guests of the owner. Southern hospitality dripped all over us.

We drove back to Jackson that morning. It being Christmas Day, when we arrived back in Evers' suburban neighborhood, all kids were out playing with their Christmas toys, the weather having cooperated with an 80-degree inducement. I saw one bike and one scooter. The rest of the toys were guns of all varieties. No dolls, no trucks, just guns. Michelle Gregory picked us off, from behind a fire hydrant, as we turned the corner, with a gun that "twanged" and produced real smoke.

A frightening tradition in holiday vogue in Mississippi, is the igniting of fireworks. Christmas in Mississippi is a totally militaristic atmosphere. Had Santa been on the street corners in Jackson, he would have no doubt had kids ask for "a gun like Daddy's and six cartons of firecrackers," or fireworks to throw at crackers.

The most terrifying feeling in the world is to walk down the street expecting to get shot, and to hear a volley of explosions. More than once, in the company of the General, I thought I was directly on the firing line, only to discover some kids playing with their Christmas toys.

That night we drove up to Delta country, Clarksdale, for a benefit. The Delta region being what it is, all necessary precautions were taken. Our motorcade was made up of three cars, all amply supplied with bodyguards and ammunition. Evers drove the lead car, equipped with a walkie-talkie and four protectors. The General, Lil, and I were in the middle car, driven by our bodyguard. The rear car was completely filled with a protection crew and a walkie-talkie. The lead and rear cars were in constant communication.

The driver placed his .38 on the seat beside him, and told me to slip out the bullets if we were stopped. Then he gave careful instructions to put the revolver back on the seat—out in the open—and to not try and hide it. In Mississippi, your weapon must be in plain sight, or you will get busted for having a concealed weapon. None of this sneaky killing for Mississippi law.

When we arrived in Clarksdale, a friendly car guided us to the church where the rally was being held. An appreciative crowd of turkey consumers awaited us. Also waiting was Ben Collins, the local police chief. Dr. Aaron

Henry, who headed the Mississippi Freedom Democratic party in Atlantic City, was in charge of the program. He introduced Mrs. Peas, who told the audience what the day of distribution had meant to the Delta people:

"When we saw the truck arrive with those big fat turkey hens, it was unbelievable. We've done without that kind of food on Christmas for a long time. And the white folks sent Mr. Gregory some possums. Well, they can just send him all they want, in season and out of season, and he can send them back to us, and we'll eat 'em. Christmas is better this year, because there were turkeys on tables that never had one before. Two nights before Thanksgiving, Mr. Gregory said, 'If I get you the turkeys, can you eat 'em?' Well, we ate them, didn't we?" And the congregation shouted, "Amen!"

Ed Davis spoke in his Harlem street corner vernacular. Only, his ideas would have been very unfamiliar to anyone who had heard him in his home territory. He was talking like an *integrationist*. The General got his conversion!

Dick Gregory, of course, had the last word: "Don't ever give up. The white man knows you're tryin' to vote the gun out of his hand, and he won't let go easily. *But this isn't a struggle of black against white, it's right against wrong*. And wrong have never defeated right in all history."

There was victory written on the faces of those applauding. We sang "We Shall Overcome."

Dick Gregory's airlift had been a success. But the Christmas joy of the nation was literally dampened by the floods which devastated the entire Northwest. Mississippi Governor Paul Johnson was quoted as saying, "I am sure the people of Mississippi would appreciate it very much if those turkeys were sent to the Northwest disaster area."

The General chuckled. "We got them turkeys from out West," he said. "Now how they gonna cook them under ten feet of water?" And then he added, "We can't handle those problems that God has inflicted upon man, like that Northwest disaster; we're trying to solve some of those that *man* has inflicted upon man."

Dick Gregory is fond of saying, "these are trying times, not normal times." And indeed many painful moments are yet to be in the social revolution that is sweeping this country. When these moments of crisis erupt, I am sure Dick Gregory will be there. He will be there because true brotherhood is the dominant concern of his life. Those who have seen Dick Gregory in nightclub performances will remember his parting words to his laughing audience:

"I'm gonna leave now. I'm not going to tell you to be your brother's keeper. If you can't learn to be your brother's brother, you'll never keep him well. So good night, God bless you, and may Nature have fun with you."

THE SHADOW THAT SCARES ME

I

You will know the truth, and the truth will make you free.

JOHN 8:32

YOU WILL KNOW THE TRUTH

When I stand in the pulpit to speak and look out into the faces of those good church folks, I am always reminded of the old spiritual, "Were you there when they crucified my Lord?" When church people sing those words, they have an expression on their faces which suggests they *would* have been there—on the Hill of the Skull standing at the foot of the cross—if they had the chance. But it is so cheap and easy to sing about what you *would* do two thousand years too late. It is time to talk about what you *will* do and *are* doing right now.

God is nothing more, or less, than truth. So let us begin to tell the truth, especially in church. The Gospel of John suggests that telling the truth is the way to really worship God. And Jesus said that the truth will make us free. Not until we are willing to tell the whole truth can we expect to be free. When we were marching nonviolently and the truth was being crucified in the streets of this nation today, were you there? When your children and grandchildren read about the current struggle for human dignity in their history books, what will be your answer when they look into your eyes and ask, "Were you there?"

And if the Russians or the Chinese took over this country in the morning and issued a decree that anyone attending religious services would be mowed down with a machine gun, would you be there in church? Perhaps you would. I believe many Negroes would lay down their lives for their church. But there is one thing those same Negroes would *not* do. They would not wear a freedom button on their jobs in front of white folks!

As long as we are telling the truth about freedom, let me make an honest confession. I am almost beginning to love George Wallace. He is a man who came up North and proved to northerners what Negroes have known all their lives and been afraid to say. He proved to the nation that the system of oppression over black people does not begin south of the Mason-Dixon line. It really begins south of the Canadian border. George Wallace sat on national television, on *Face the Nation*, and showed pictures of police brutality; of cops riding horses into crowds of teen-age demonstrators; of nightsticks being used to break up demonstrations. And all of these pictures were taken in northern cities. For more than a hundred years it has been popular to put the blame for the racial situation in this country on the southern white brother. The southerner has been accused over and over again in all sorts of heinous ways.

But let us tell the truth long enough to realize who sold the black man into slavery. Northerners controlled the ships which were used to bring us to these shores from Africa. We were sold by a northern white man to a southern white man. Then the northern white man got slick one day and turned to his southern brother, after he had pocketed the money, and said, "Get rid of your slaves." The southerner should have said, "Do I get a refund?" The storekeeper will give you two cents back on a Coke bottle, if the bottle belongs to you!

We have been so unfair to that southerner. When the federal government finally decides that the Mississippi schools must be integrated, we stand by and watch them send a gun and a soldier to the South to force Mississippi to integrate. When we get ready to try to integrate the schools in Chicago or New York City, they give us a bus to transport a few children from one segregated neighborhood to another. If a gun and a soldier are appropriate for the southern white brother, the same standard should apply to the North.

On the opening day of school in the fall of 1964, school after school was integrated in Jackson, Mississippi, without any kind of incident. The same day in Jackson Heights, Queens, in liberal old New York City, sixty-five screaming white mothers, with their babies in their arms, were arrested for opposing the new school integration plan. For too long the South has been viewed as the garbage can of race relations. No matter what happened to point out northern injustices, people have always looked to the South and said, "See how much worse it is down there." But now the brother in the South is putting the lid tightly on that racial garbage can and there is no place for northerners to dump their garbage except in their own backyard. And the stink is beginning to spread all over the North.

Once when I was in Selma, Alabama, a colored cat called me up and asked, "Would you come over to the station and be on my television show?" In Selma, Alabama, in 1964, a Negro had his own television show from eight o'clock in the morning until twelve noon. How many Negroes have their own television shows on stations in the North? Mississippi radio stations have colored disc jockeys playing soul music. And these are major network stations. In the North, if you hear a colored disc jockey, you can bet it is an all-colored station and you are not going to hear the stock market report on that same station.

Over the past fifty years, most of the top athletes in northern colleges have been Negroes; in the Big Ten, the

Ivy League, and the West Coast Conference. Yet there has not been one Negro head coach or one Negro referee in those conferences. That is a disgrace. If you drew up a list of the outstanding Negroes in this country, you would find that 98 percent have been educated in southern segregated schools. For when that southern white brother gave the Negro an all-black school, he also gave him black teachers and a black principal. At a very early age, the southern Negro student was able to see black folks in authority and could identify with achievement. Up North, 99.9 percent of the schools have white principals and the Negro student must identify with the colored janitor.

The Revolution of Right Against Wrong

There is a great social revolution going on in America today. And the wonderful thing about this revolution is that it is not black against white. It is simply right against wrong. You only realize this truth when you are on the front line of the struggle for human dignity. There are many white folks who hate civil rights demonstrators. But if they really knew the truth, they would love those of us on the front line. White folks should really dislike the Negroes who sit back and do nothing but tell them what they want to hear, while all the time hating white folks' guts.

If the closest you ever get to the front line struggle is the Huntley-Brinkley Report on television, you will never know the truth. On that television news report, the Negro who is not on the front line sees a dog biting his little black cousin or a white cop knocking his grandma down to the ground. Quite naturally his invisible hatred for white folks comes boiling to the surface. But the cameras fail to show all those white kids getting knocked down also. The television cameras were not around to show that white sheriff who came into the jail, tore off his badge and threw it to the ground, with tears in his eyes, because he just couldn't stand being wrong any longer. You only see these beautiful sights on the front line of action, but this is the truth about freedom and dignity in this social revolution.

The television cameras are not able to portray the *real* truth. They cannot capture the strange truth that ten minutes after we are arrested and thrown into the jail, we *own* that jail. When a man is jailed for doing right, suddenly the jail becomes the prisoner. The people behind the bars are in control and the prison guards are the slaves of wrongdoing. This is a revolution of right against wrong. And wrong has never ultimately won out against right in the history of the world.

The day you join the revolution is the day you will quit hating. The only people who hate the Germans or the Japanese today are those who stayed home during the war. The soldiers on the front line married the "enemy" after the war was over, because there is no hatred on the front line. And Negroes who never joined the struggle for human dignity are the ones who will be shooting white folks in the streets, because they are hating more and more every day. I know this truth because I have been physically beaten by Negroes who tell me that I have been bought by the white man because I preach non-violence.

We have gone into towns to demonstrate and Negro ministers have refused to let us use their churches as freedom schools. I have to wonder how we can go down-town to picket the white brother when there are so many of our own brothers who are wrong. A man does not have to be white to wear a sheet or black to wear a freedom button. It is time to expose Negroes who are holding us back and put a sheet over their heads. Ours is not a struggle of black against white, but of right against wrong. When we know this truth, we are on our way to freedom.

The Soldiers and the 4-F's

What is hurting this revolution most of all is the 4-F's who sit back and do nothing. Then when the struggle is over, the 4-F's receive the GI Bill. Never before in the history of revolutions has this happened, but it is happening to us. The Negro attorney who says, "Demonstrations are hurting our cause," becomes the first Negro prosecuting attorney, after the suffering and the bleeding are over. The Negro doctor who tells white folks what they want to hear, who says we should not be extreme in demonstrating, becomes the first colored public health commissioner, after his brothers on the front line have been jailed and beaten.

I went to the Auto Show in Chicago in 1964 and it brought tears to my eyes. It was the biggest Auto Show of the year anywhere in the country. And many of the fashion models were Negro! The year before there were *no* Negro models. Seeing all of those beautiful black models made me sick to my stomach. Because I knew who had gotten them their jobs. It was the sister on the front line. You saw her in every demonstration that was covered by the television camera crews. She was that short, black, nappy-haired girl being bitten by the dogs. She couldn't win a beauty contest in her own living room with her momma as the judge! But she got those Negro models their jobs at the Auto Show. And yet if you asked one of those models to come out to the front line of action, or even to pick up a picket sign, she would look at you as if you were a fool. The 4-F's are getting all of the GI Bill.

I remember demonstrating in Atlanta, Georgia, in 1963. It was a long hard struggle, with minimum participation by local Negroes, but we finally integrated seventeen restaurants. After the struggle was over, I looked so disgusted that the white restaurant owner asked me, "What's wrong, Gregory?" And I told him, "I just wish I could give you a picture of each one of us demonstrators who faced the dogs, had hot water thrown on us, and went to jail to force you to open your doors to everyone. I would ask you to hang those pictures over your cash register. And if a Negro walked into your restaurant whose picture was not on the wall, I would ask you not to serve him. Tell him to integrate a restaurant for himself."

This is the greatest revolution in history because of the soldiers fighting the battle. They are like no other soldiers who ever fought. There are Negroes on the front line who will lay down their lives demonstrating in front of a new housing development. Yet they know that after the victory is won, the only person who can move into that new development is Ralph Bunche. That front line soldier in the battle for human dignity will demonstrate in front of a hospital to get more Negro doctors on the staff. If the administrator of the hospital came out to the picket line and offered that soldier a job, he couldn't take it; because he didn't even finish grade school. But he is laying down his life for his brother. This front line soldier in the battle for right lives by the true spirit of God, "I am my brother's keeper." Beyond that, the front line soldier in the struggle for human dignity is trying to create a nation where each man is his brother's brother. This struggle is not black against white.

We were demonstrating in Chicago in 1964 and the cops

started pushing and shoving. After I walked off the front line of demonstration, a Negro cop followed me, winking and blinking, and said, "Hey, brother. I didn't mean to shove you just now, but my job is at stake. I'm a colored cop." Not until he said he was a "colored cop" did I get mad. I told him, "I defy you to make this revolution black against white. When you shoved us on the steps of city hall just now, you were a cop like all the rest of them. But since you want to be a colored cop, let me tell you why you cannot mess up our revolution. I have seen the white sheriff throw down his badge because he couldn't take any more. I saw the white farmer in Birmingham, Alabama, throw down his hose rather than spray little black kids. He was arrested by his racist brothers. I had some respect for you when you were just a cop. But when you try to beg off because of being a colored cop, I have no respect at all. Because you are trying to inject racism into our revolution."

The Black Racists

If we are going to *know* the truth which makes us free, we must *tell* the truth about racism. White folks are not the only racists in the country today. Black folks are racist also. And their racism is not only directed toward white folks, but also against other Negroes. I do a comedy routine about moving into a white neighborhood. The first day I receive some callers on my front porch. Not the white racists, but the colored delegation. Dr. Jones standing there with his lips tucked in. The delegation has come by to make sure I act right and don't embarrass them in this white neighborhood. Dr. Jones says, "You have to watch yourself out here and remember the white folks are watching us." And I say, "What are you doin', stealin' or something?"

Sophisticated Negroes are embarrassed by the actions of their poor black brother in the ghetto, but are not embarrassed by the actions of poor whites in their ghetto. That is racism. But it is not a Negroid characteristic. It is the normal result of living under a system of oppression. After a period of time, the oppressed man begins imitating the behavior of the oppressor. It was not uncommon in the concentration camps of World War II for the Jewish prisoners to imitate the Nazi soldiers when their backs were turned. Some of the Jewish prisoners would cut their clothes in the same way the German uniforms were fashioned. They would misuse fellow prisoners in the manner of their Nazi oppressors. Imitating the behavior of the oppressor is a way of escaping one's own oppression. Negroes who have made a few advances within the system of oppression are frequently prejudiced toward other Negroes whose behavior reminds them of the worst the oppressive system has to offer.

If I had to choose between losing my wife to a white man and losing her to a black man, I would choose the black man, because I would not want to face the embarrassment of my friends reminding me that a white man stole my wife. Yet I know I am making a racist choice. A simple illustration will show the extent to which unconscious racism victimizes every human being in this country. My secretary and I boarded a plane in Chicago on our way to Newark. The plane was crowded and there were no two seats together available. My secretary took one single seat and I took another. I happened to be sitting next to a white woman and we began talking about the social problems of America. I mentioned that I thought the number one problem in America was racism. She was visibly relieved to hear me say this and she said, "You are so right. You know, I wanted to get up and give the young lady who is with you my seat. But I was afraid you would think I didn't want to sit next to you."

Suppose two airplanes took off at the same time; one filled with white passengers and the other filled with black passengers. If you had to decide which plane would crash, what would your choice be? Most white folks will choose the all-black plane and most Negroes will choose the all-white plane. That is racism. If it is not possible to save the good Negroes and the good white folks in each plane, then they should both go down. Whenever a man's color becomes the basic factor in the choices of life, it is racism.

There are many critics of the struggle for human dignity, both black and white. These critics are fond of saying that certain kinds of demonstrations only hurt the Negro's cause. Such a statement is like saying you are giving too much medicine to a dead man. Even President Johnson has criticized certain forms of protest. But if he and Lady Bird woke up one morning as black as my wife and me, they would both sign up for the next demonstration!

So many people criticized the stall-in in New York City on the opening day of the World's Fair. They said we were going too far. People used to ask me, "Where did they ever get such a crazy, wild idea of running out of gas on the expressways?" The answer is simple; from watching all those cars run out of gas on that TV commercial. I can easily justify the stall-in. If the senior citizens of this country, our Senators and Congressmen, can hold a stall-in in the sacred halls of Congress debating civil rights legislation, and call it a "filibuster," we second class citizens can hold a stall-in on a dirty American highway.

The critics also say we should take our problem to court and fight the battle legally. I tried that and it didn't work. How can I get justice in a court where the judge is an elected official whose votes come out of an all-white neighborhood? When the judge knows he will have to have voter approval to get reelected, he cannot have an open and sympathetic ear for my problem.

And how can I get justice from a judge who honestly does not know that he is prejudiced? For example, many rich Negroes have gotten divorces in northern courts, but you have never read where a colored woman has gotten a large settlement from her rich colored husband. Yet the rich white man better not lose his wife or she gets all his money. So how is this judge going to give me justice when he can't even treat my woman right?

The courts and society have never treated my woman right. If my wife goes downtown and steals something, when she is caught she is called a hoodlum. If a white celebrity's wife gets caught stealing, she is a kleptomaniac. The black woman is listed with the crime rate and the white woman is placed on the sick list.

A white man and his wife can go to court and get a divorce. Say he is making fifty thousand dollars a year and they have three children. The court grants the wife custody of the children. If she marries another white man who is making fifty thousand dollars a year, do you think the father could go back into court and get custody of his children because his wife married again? Not a chance. But if I married her he could do just that. Such is the racism of the American court. I cannot take my problem there.

How Fair Can the Black Man Be?

The critics say that the Negro is expecting too much too fast. Extreme demonstrations involving civil disobedience are condemned as an example of how unfair the Negro is being. He cannot expect freedom overnight. The history of the Negro in America is a study in patience and trying to be fair. Negroes did not want to get out into the streets to demonstrate their problem. They were so busy trying to be fair. For over a hundred years white America told the Negro to try to raise himself up to the white man's standards and he would get his freedom. And in fairness the Negro tried. Slaves didn't wear good clothes or shoes, but we tried to meet that standard. We put on the white man's shoes, his socks, his underwear, his shirt and his tie. But that wasn't enough and we still didn't get our freedom.

In our effort to be fair, we thought the problem must be our physical appearance. So we grew a mustache and tried to cover up our thick lips. Still no freedom. We thought nappy hair must be the hang-up. So we got processes and straightened out the hair problem. Over a hundred-year period, we have gone from the bottom of our feet to the top of our heads trying to be fair. Finally we ran out of things to do to try to please white America and we were driven into the streets.

How fair can the black man be? Think about all those black women in the South who raised those white boys who ended up lynching their sons. And still they cooked and cared for their sons' murderers, taking comfort only in the thought, "The Lord will take care of them. Vengeance is mine saith the Lord." A person cannot be any more fair than that. When you stop to consider how long Negroes have been controlling the white folks' kitchen, you realize how fair we have been. Negroes have prepared every bite white America put into its mouth. If Negroes had wanted to be vicious enough to seek revenge, one well-organized poison campaign would have drastically altered the ethnic balance.

Think about that slave couple, especially those of you

who have children. Close your eyes and imagine yourself a slave. Your wife comes to you and tells you she is pregnant. Visualize the slave couple falling to their knees in prayer, begging God Almighty that their child be born deformed so that he might be free from being sold on the slave block. Imagine being the victim of a society so vicious that your child could be sold not only to another slave master but taken to another state. How would you feel?

The slave couple would pitifully petition the Lord God to grant that their baby be born without an arm or a leg, so that he could escape the labor of the fields. Sometimes the prayer was answered and the baby was born deformed. And the black woman would look at the black man, with tears of joy streaming down her face, and exclaim, "Our prayer has been answered. Our baby was born deformed." Can you see both of them falling to their knees in a prayer of thanks; thanking their God for blessing them with a deformed child? How fair can the black man be? It is an unwritten law that a man who destroys another man's home shall inherit the wind.

I remember when we were demonstrating to integrate public accommodations, the restaurant owner told us to be fair. He said his place of business belonged to him; he opened it with his hard-earned money and he insisted he had the right to serve anyone he chose to serve. I was glad to tell that white restaurant owner, "Good brother, you don't have to serve me." But I had to remind him also that it is my tax money which pays the public health commissioner to license his restaurant. My tax dollars are used to pay the fireman who comes to protect his establishment when the skillet gets too hot. My tax dollars pay the cop who guards the restaurant while the day's receipts are being counted. If a man wants a restaurant to himself and his friends, let him hire his own health commissioner, his own cop, and his own fireman. Then he can have his crummy joint. But the day is over when I will allow my tax money to be spent protecting a place which will not serve me, but any nontax paying white foreigner can come in and use the air conditioning while sipping a mint julep out of a glass I made sure was inspected. That is how fair I am willing to be.

The Truth About Freedom

In fairness to America, we must tell the truth about freedom. White and black youth are drafted into the armed services to be the defenders of truth and freedom in Vietnam. But the truth about freedom must be told in *this* country before it can be represented on foreign shores. How can I be asked to go to Vietnam to fight for the "instant freedom" of the Vietnamese, when my own black kids at home must get their freedom on the installment plan? It does not make sense to require a black youth to sacrifice his life to guarantee a foreigner a better way of life than his own parents have in America. Back home the black soldier's parents will hear people say, "Education is the problem. Freedom for the Negro in America depends upon raising his educational standard." But no one has ever questioned the Vietnamese educational standard. If the educational standard is not a question in granting freedom to the Vietnamese, America had better stop questioning mine.

America requires a Negro soldier from Mississippi to go to Vietnam and chase a Vietcong through the bushes trying to kill him. Yet it is a crime in America for that same Negro to chase a Mississippi Ku Klux Klaner through the swamps of Mississippi trying to kill him. On the battlefield of Vietnam, the Negro soldier only has to worry about losing his own life; the fight is between himself and the Vietcong. Back home, this racist in America will not only kill that Negro soldier, but wipe out his whole family and blow up his church. Yet it is a crime *not* to go to Vietnam and kill the Vietcong and also a crime *to* kill the racist in America who will wipe out a whole family. That is the insane truth about freedom.

It is not only the black soldier who sees the contradictions about freedom displayed on the Vietnam battlefield. Eighteen- and nineteen-year-old young men, white and black, are required to go to Vietnam to lay down their lives to secure the right to vote for the Vietnamese. When those soldiers return to their America, they must wait two or three years before they can exercise their own right to vote. They are old enough to die for another man's right to vote, but too young to vote themselves.

The white soldier will suffer, bleed, and die for the rights of a colored Vietnamese. Then the soldier comes home to Cicero, Philadelphia, or Memphis. If the same colored Vietnamese, whom the white soldier was willing to die for, tried to move next door to him in America, many white veterans would point the gun at their would-be colored neighbors. A nation this sick cannot survive.

When America admits the truth about freedom at home, she will begin to understand her image abroad. If I were a known child molester and had served time in jail for that crime, you would not hire me to be your baby-sitter. You would know the history of my past performance when I get around children and you would not want to take a chance. Because of my record, you would not trust me. People all over the world know America's record. They know the history of America looting her land from the original native inhabitants. They continue to see the atrocities committed upon the Indian. In the eyes of the world,

America has been convicted over and over again of molesting her black children, by permitting Negroes to be lynched and civil rights workers to be gunned down in the streets. Is it any wonder that countries all over the world do not trust America, with her record of man's inhumanity to man, to baby-sit for their freedom?

Those who are opposed to freedom always resist the truth. Consider the number of churches that have been blown up or burned to the ground in the South. Negroes and liberal-minded white folks consider such acts terrible atrocities. When human lives are lost in the destruction of a church, it is a tragedy. But the destruction of the church itself is not tragic. When the church building is destroyed, religion is forced out into the street where it should have been all along!

The Syndicate and the Ku Klux Klan

The reason why churches were destroyed in the South is because ministers finally started telling the truth about freedom. For years southern ministers have been afraid to speak out. The Ku Klux Klan has always been able to terrify and intimidate the southern Negro. One day the minister developed enough backbone to overcome his fear, climb into his pulpit, and tell the truth about the Klan. He called the names of Klan members and openly identified the law-enforcement officers and the businessmen hiding under those hoods. The minister traced the route of Klan violence. As a result, his church was destroyed the next morning. Those who are opposed to freedom always resist the truth.

But this is not a southern phenomenon. If the northern minister, priest or rabbi would stand in his pulpit one morning and call the names of the top men in the crime syndicate; if he would trace the syndicate's reefer route and tell the truth about dope traffic, violence, and prostitution, that northern clergyman's church would be destroyed also.

The syndicate has the same grip of fear on the North as the Klan has always had on the South. The syndicate has burned more restaurants in Chicago than the Klan has burned churches in Mississippi. The syndicate killed more people in Chicago in eighteen months than the Klan lynched in Mississippi in two years. These acts of violence go unnoticed by the same people who decry southern atrocities.

People in the North will see a man shot down in the street with a machine gun. If they know the syndicate is behind the killing, they are afraid to appear in court as a witness. They know what the reprisals will be. Yet those same fear-ridden people cannot understand how the Klan gets by with their acts of violence. Opponents of truth use fear to create a climate of silence. Until that silence is shattered by the open and fearless speaking of the truth all over this country, no man is free.

The White Man's Slavery

The free man is the man with no fears. The strange truth in America today is that the Negro has become the psychological master and the white man the psychological slave. It is the mark of the slave to be afraid. Since he is not a free man, he is the victim of fear. The master has no fears. The slave runs and hides.

When a Negro family moves into an all-white neighborhood, white residents begin running. Immediately the "For Sale" signs appear in the front lawn of every house on the block. Who is free? If I went on the Ed Sullivan Show tonight and spoke in favor of integrated marriages, nothing would happen to me. If Ed Sullivan spoke in favor of the same thing, he would lose his rating and his job. Who is free?

If I have a white friend who needs a place to stay, I can give him my keys and let him use my apartment as long as he likes. My neighbors will think nothing of his being in my home, even if my wife and kids are home and I am away. The white man in America today cannot give me his keys or let me use his apartment without every white neighbor in the block being outraged. If he is away from the apartment and I am alone with his wife, the neighbors will automatically assume I am doing something sexually with her. Who is free?

I was on a radio show not long ago. It was one of those talk shows which encouraged listeners to telephone in their opinions. A lady phoned to speak with me while I was on the air. She identified herself as being white and said, "I am sorry I can't give you my name. I just wanted you to know that I agree with you." She agreed with me; but her color and the reactions of her friends and neighbors who might be listening to the same program kept her from mentioning her own name. Who is free? Only the psychological slave hides from his own name!

One of my white neighbors revealed his psychological slavery to me one day. We live in the same apartment building and have daughters the same age. We send our children to the University of Chicago Lab School. My white neighbor came to me one day mentally upset and said, "Greg, I have to talk to you." He told me that he had gone to pick up his little four-year-old daughter at school. She came out of the school with her arm around a little Negro boy. When my neighbor saw this, all of a sudden it dawned on him that he did not want his daughter to marry a Negro. This sudden realization upset him and he wanted to talk to me about it.

I looked into that white man's eyes and said, "My little daughter is freer than your daughter. She can marry a gorilla if she wants to." But the frightening recognition was that this white man, with all of his education and wealth, was such a psychological slave that he could look at a little four-year-old child and worry about whom she will be having sexual intercourse with one day. What kind of mental slavery will cause a man to rob his own daughter of her childhood? Who can think of a four-year-old kid being married? I would never consider worrying about whom my daughter will marry until she is close to marriageable age. The only thing I worry about now is how much money I am paying for those funny-looking pictures she draws in Lab School.

The psychological slave has allowed himself to be mentally victimized by his own fears. Does it not seem strange that after all these years of being called "nigger" Negroes have never developed a word just as vicious for white folks? In most cases the white man will not be hit by a Negro if he calls him "nigger." If the white man calls the Negro a "bastard," he might have a fight on his hands. But he will usually get no physical reaction from "nigger." Somehow nature instinctively teaches you who to hit and who to feel sorry for.

The Negro has refused to allow himself to be psychologically enslaved. I am Dick Gregory; I live in America; I am a Negro. I am an individual first, an American second, and a Negro third. If a man calls me a nigger, he is calling me something I am not. The nigger exists only in his own mind; therefore his mind is the nigger. I must feel sorry for such a man.

If I looked at a television set and called it an ice-cream cone, the ice-cream cone would exist only in my own mind. My mind becomes the ice-cream cone. A white sheriff called me a "monkey" one day. A monkey has straight hair, thin lips, and blue eyes. Anyone can look at me and tell I don't fit that description. The sheriff is the monkey because the "monkey-image" exists only in his own mind. He has become the psychological slave; the victim of his own fears.

Only the truth will make men free. The psychological slave will never be free until he knows the truth about his fears. The Negro in America will never be free until he tells white America the absolute truth, however painful that truth might be for both whites and blacks. There is one way the truth could create instant freedom for all people. If some strange, stubborn, many-headed creature from outer space landed on this earth one day and addressed us all as "Earth People," he would be speaking the truth. For we are *all* earth people. Nations all over the world would set aside their petty differences and sit down at the conference table to decide how to deal with this strange creature from outer space; this creature who has spoken the truth about us all. World cooperation and universal brotherhood would become an instantaneous reality.

The Wintertime Soldier

Today the truth is being spoken and lived by the wintertime soldier in the great moral revolution for human dignity. The wintertime soldier is the man who struggles for truth and freedom when all the odds are against him. George Washington headed a band of wintertime soldiers. He inspired them to march on Christmas Eve against the British in spite of overwhelming odds. George Washington used the words of Tom Paine to give strength and courage to his wintertime soldiers. And those words echo today as an ode to freedom and truth for all men everywhere. Tom Paine said: "These are times that try men's souls. The summer soldier and the sunshine patriot will, in this crisis, shrink from the service of their country; but he that stands it *now*, deserves the love and thanks of man and woman. Tyranny, like hell, is not easily conquered; yet we have this consolation with us, that the harder the conflict, the more glorious the triumph. What we obtain too cheap, we esteem too lightly. If there be trouble, let it be in my day that my children may have peace. It is dearness only that gives everything its value. Heaven knows how to put a proper price upon its goods; and it would be strange indeed if so celestial an article as *freedom* should not be highly rated."

II

And the tongue is a fire. . . . With it we bless the Lord and Father, and with it we curse men, who are made in the likeness of God. From the same mouth come blessing and cursing. My brethren, this ought not to be so.

JAMES 3:6, 9–10

AMERICA IS MY MOMMA

The Apostle James describes well what I have experienced in the church all my life. The tongue, the words we say or sing and do not mean, and the verses of scripture we interpret to fit our own prejudices, stains the whole body and sets on fire the cycle of nature. The same words are used to praise God and to curse men; to justify evil and to condemn it.

A popular song in the church is "The Battle Hymn of the Republic." Really listen to the words of that song and you will realize that very few people have the right to sing it. The day a person does decide to sing it should be the last day of his life. That is what the words of the song imply: "As He died to make men holy, let us die to make men free." If the Enforcer swept through the church today and said, "Put up or shut up," I only know about five folks who could sing that song and mean it. And three of them are already dead.

"As He died to make men holy, let us die to make men free." We do just the reverse. We will try to *kill* to make men free. But the song doesn't say that. It says, "Let us *die* to make men free." This refusal to live by our words makes a laughingstock out of the church, Good Friday, and Easter. Another song which amuses me is "Onward, Christian Soldiers." Church folks seem to think a Christian soldier is a Marine who prays. When you sing, "Onward,

Christian Soldiers," you are not *really* talking about a man who will follow the cause of right to his death.

The church today has become a sick comedy. I tell my own kids to go to church only as a form of entertainment. The church is in such sad condition today that I cannot justify their attendance for any other reason. If my momma had told me that the church was a form of entertainment, I could have understood those old sisters sitting in the front pew of my church looking so evil. We never had a picture of the Devil in my house; only pictures of Jesus. But if we had a picture of the Devil, I'm sure it would have looked like one of those front pew sisters.

Take a Prostitute to Church

The church is supposed to be so pure, much more pure than the nightclub. Yet I can take a prostitute to the nightclub with me and nobody will automatically assume I have been sleeping with her. It isn't strange to see a prostitute in a nightclub and she is welcome. My wife can walk into the nightclub with a pimp and nobody will assume she has been sleeping with him. But I defy you women to pick up an old wino out of the gutter on your way to church some Sunday and bring him along with you to hear the message of God. When you arrive, just listen to the sisters whisper.

And you men, I defy you to invite the town prostitute some Sunday morning, "Sister, would you like to come with me to church and hear my minister?" If she accepts the invitation, the minute you walk in the front door people will start whispering that you must have been with her all night. This is the church. It doesn't happen in a nightclub, a pool hall or a tavern. It makes me think they put the crosses on the wrong buildings.

Why Judas?

When I was a kid, I used to ask my momma why the church accused a Jew of killing Christ. In Sunday school they taught me that all Judas did was *kiss* Christ. I asked, "Momma, if you kiss me on the cheek and Daddy takes a gun and pulls the trigger on me, who are they going to get for murder?" Momma answered, "Daddy, of course." That bothered me, because I could not understand why the Good Book kept accusing the kisser. Why not get that Roman soldier's name; the one with the nails and the hammer. He is the real killer. Just as it is today, nobody ever wants to accuse the man with the gun.

Of course, Momma knew her Bible and she had an explanation. She said, "They didn't know what Jesus looked like and if Judas hadn't kissed him, he couldn't have been arrested. That is why Judas gets blamed for killing Christ." The story I learned in Sunday school did not say that Christ was invisible. He walked out in the open every day. Thousands of people saw him and heard him teach. Two thousand years later we have his picture on the wall and claim to know what he looked like. We don't have pictures of Judas.

So I said to Momma, "Do you mean to tell me that the king and the queen, who own the Army, the Navy, the CIA, and the secret police, were so stupid that they didn't know what the boss looked like but they could recognize his helper?" If you can believe that, you can believe anything. The power structure had enough sense to know that if Jesus had lived he would have hurt them. But they didn't know what he looked like. Even as a child that explanation didn't make sense to me.

When you start twisting the words of the Bible around, the church and the whole world are in trouble. The Christian soldiers are pictured on the front page of the newspaper with their heads bowed worshiping with the chaplain immediately after a good kill. The Christian soldier prays to his God. His buddy on the other side of the firing line, called the "enemy," prays to his God. And they are both praying at the same time! Man really puts God on the spot on the front line of the battlefield.

If I was silly enough to go to war, I would give God better treatment than that. I wouldn't take a Bible to battle with me and I wouldn't pray. My last prayer would be just before I shipped out. I would tell God, "Okay, Brother. I am going to do for myself for about four or five years. You'll hear from me when I get back."

When I was a kid, religion made con-men out of everyone in our house. I flatly refused to pray the Lord's Prayer. It just did not make sense to pray to God, "Give us this day our daily bread," when sometimes there was six months' food supply in the pantry. I used to listen to my momma pray. She would start out with the Lord's Prayer. Since everything is really covered in that prayer, she should have stopped while she was ahead. But she would start improvising. She would pray, "Bless the sick and shut-in," which she knew she wasn't going to visit, and then she would start her thirty-minute beg. "Lord, you know the rent is due, the bills have to be paid; and if you will just do *this* for me, let me tell you what I'll do for *you*."

Hearing a prayer like that used to make me wonder who God is. Momma would always try to work out deals with Him. But at the end of every prayer, Momma would always give God a cop-out: "Lord, let not my will but thine be done." Next week the rent still would be due and Momma would say, "I guess the Lord knew what He was doing." On those church radio services I heard prayers which were even safer. I heard a woman pray, "Lord, thank you for all the good you have done to me and the evil too." That *really* made me wonder who God is. It is a vicious God whom you have to thank for wrong.

I finally came to the conclusion that I couldn't go to school and to church too. At school I would be taught to prove everything to the *n*th degree. When I asked questions in church, looking for proof, the minister would say, "What's wrong with you, boy?" So I decided if I had to go to church, I would make some money at it. Back in the 1940's when I was a kid, my church used to take up a special collection every Sunday for African missionary work. The church didn't even have a back wall in it yet and there was much more work to do on the building, so I knew the money was not going to Africa. I used to sneak back and wipe out that collection every Sunday. It was the only way I could justify spending my time in church when they wouldn't explain things to me.

Joseph and Mary at the Hilton

I never could understand the story of Christmas. People used to weep and wail every year over the fact that "there was no room for Mary in the inn." Every Christmas the innkeeper took a beating in my church for the way he treated poor Mary and Joseph. But Mary was pregnant. Suppose Mary and Joseph came back today and walked into the lobby of the Conrad Hilton and said to the desk clerk, "This is Mary and I am Joseph. We're not married, but let me tell you about this dream we had." You know they would be thrown out immediately. The dream might be legitimate, but you don't tell the desk clerk about it and then get mad because he doesn't believe you. You can't go into a hotel today with a pregnant woman to have a baby. Nor can you check into the hospital just to have a place to sleep. It is just the reverse. You go to the hospital to have the baby and go to the hotel to read the Bible—there is one in every room. The government has taken the Bibles out of the schools, but it left them in the hotel rooms. So maybe the government knows which place is more hip.

My momma could never understand how white folks could twist the words of the Bible around to justify racial segregation. Yet she could read the Ten Commandments, which clearly say, "Thou shalt not kill," and still justify eating meat. Momma couldn't read the newspaper very well, but she sure could interpret the Word of God. "God meant you shouldn't kill people," she used to say. But I insisted, "Momma, he didn't say that. He said, 'Thou shalt not kill.' If you leave that statement alone, a whole lot of things would be safe from killing. But if you are going to twist the words about killing to mean what you want them to mean, then let white folks do the same thing with justifying racial segregation."

"You can't live without eating meat," Momma would persist. "You'd starve." I couldn't buy that either. You get milk from a cow without killing it. You do not have to kill an animal to get what you need from it. You get wool from the sheep without killing it. Two of the strongest animals in the jungle are vegetarians—the elephant and the gorilla. The first two years are the most important years of a man's life, and during that period he is not involved with eating meat. If you suddenly become very ill, there is a good chance you will be taken off a meat diet. So it is a myth that killing is necessary for survival. The day I decide that I must have a piece of steak to nourish my body, I will also give the cow the same right to nourish herself on human beings.

There is so little basic difference between animals and humans. The process of reproduction is the same for chickens, cattle, and humans. If suddenly the air stopped circulating on the earth, or the sun collided with the earth, animals and humans would die alike. A nuclear holocaust will wipe out all life. Life in the created order is basically the same and should be respected as such. It seems to me the Bible says it is wrong to kill—period.

If we can justify *any* kind of killing in the name of religion, the door is opened for all kinds of other justifications. The fact of killing animals is not as frightening as our human tendency to justify it—to kill and not even be aware that we are taking life. It is sobering to realize that when you misuse one of the least of Nature's creatures, like the chicken, you are sowing the seed for misusing the highest of Nature's creatures, man.

If You Had to Kill Your Own Hog

Animals and humans suffer and die alike. If you had to kill your own hog before you ate it, most likely you would not be able to do it. To hear the hog scream, to see the blood spill, to see the baby being taken away from its momma, and to see the look of death in the animal's eye would turn your stomach. So you get the man at the packing house to do the killing for you. In like manner, if the wealthy aristocrats who are perpetrating conditions in the ghetto actually heard the screams of ghetto suffering, or saw the slow death of hungry little kids, or witnessed the strangulation of manhood and dignity, they could not continue the killing. But the wealthy are protected from such horror. They have people to do the killing for them. The wealthy profit from the daily murders of ghetto life but they do not see them. Those who immerse themselves in the daily life of the ghetto see the suffering—the social workers, the police, the local merchants, and the bill collectors. But the people on top never really see.

By the time you see a piece of meat in the butcher shop window, all of the blood and suffering have been washed away. When you order a steak in the restaurant, the misery has been forgotten and you see the finished product. You see a steak with butter and parsley on it. It looks appetizing and appealing and you are pleased enough to eat it. You never even consider the suffering which produced your meal or the other animals killed that day in the slaughter-house. In the same way, all the wealthy aristocrats ever see of the black community is the finished product, the window dressing, the steak on the platter—Ralph Bunche and Thurgood Marshall. The United Nations or the Supreme Court bench is the restaurant and the ghetto street corner is the slaughterhouse.

Life under ghetto conditions cuts short life expectancy. The Negro's life expectancy is shorter than the white man's. The oppressor benefits from continued oppression financially; he makes more money so that he can eat a little better. I see no difference between a man killing a chicken and a man killing a human being, by overwork and forcing ghetto conditions upon him, both so that he can eat a little better. If you can justify killing to eat meat, you can justify the conditions of the ghetto. I cannot justify either one.

Every time the white folks made my momma mad, she would grab the Bible and find something bitter in it. She would come home from the rich white folks' house, after they had just called her "nigger," or patted her on the rump or caught her stealing some steaks, open her Bible and read aloud, "It is easier for a camel to pass through the eye of a needle than for a rich man to get into Heaven." When you get involved with distorting the words of the Bible, you don't have to be bitter. The same tongue can be used to bless and curse men.

The Lord Knew There Would Be Needles

When Momma used to curse the rich white folks with the judgment against rich men, I used to try to point out the contradictions. "Momma," I would say, "they didn't have needles when the Bible was written." And she would say, "The Lord knew they would one day." Now I thought it was terribly unfair to write something that couldn't possibly be understood for a few thousand years. So I used to prod Momma for more answers. "What about those people at the time of Christ? How were they supposed to understand the Bible?" That just wasn't Momma's immediate problem. "They ain't here now," she would say. Then I would try to explain that the eye of a needle was an arch in the old Arabian cities and when a camel came through, the bigger the load the more the camel would have to stoop to get through. The rich man had more trouble getting through the eye because his load was bigger than the poor man's. But Momma wouldn't listen. She wanted *all* rich men cursed, because of what one rich man had just done to her.

Momma always had the Bible under her arm. If she was flat broke and found a nickel on the street, she would fall on her knees and say, "Thank God!" But on payday, if she found a dollar, she wouldn't even think to thank Him, because finding money didn't mean anything when there was already money in her purse. Even though the Bible clearly says, "Thou shalt not steal," Momma could always justify stealing from the white folks' pantry. She knew her kids were hungry and she used to try to justify her stealing to us. "If I didn't steal, you would starve to death. The white folks aren't paying me enough anyway." It is so easy for people to justify what they want to believe. Sophisticated Negroes today who are embarrassed by the rioting and looting in the ghetto can still justify their grandma raiding the white folks' pantry for survival. The ghetto brother is fighting for survival also. If you can justify one kind of stealing, you can justify any manifestation of theft that suits your particular fancy. But right is right and wrong is wrong.

If the same Negroes who are embarrassed by the rioting and looting in the ghetto picked up the newspaper one morning and read that the First National Bank of Kansas City was held up by five well-dressed, collegiate-looking Negroes pulling off the biggest bank robbery in history, they would not be embarrassed. They would wink at each other that morning at work and talk about how clever those cats were in Kansas City. But a Brooks Brothers suit does not change the complexion of looting. You cannot justify stealing because the thieves were brilliant and looked respectable, any more than you can justify stealing as necessary for survival. "Thou shalt not steal" means that stealing is wrong. The Bible goes further in talking about how man should treat his fellow man. It clearly condemns the conditions of life which cause a man to steal for survival. But stealing itself is still wrong. When the same tongue can bless one man's stealing and curse another man's stealing, all hell breaks loose, to paraphrase the Epistle of James!

Illegitimate Parents

My momma and my church always taught me that illegitimacy is something wrong. My society tells me that it is something "colored." Society is forever reminding me of the rate of illegitimacy in Negro neighborhoods. Statistically this is true. Negro women in America represent 20 percent of the illegitimacy rate and white women represent 2 percent. But if Negroes could ever get their hands on that white man's abortion credit card, those statistics would change.

But if illegitimacy is wrong and colored, then Christ was colored and a sinner. Because the story in the Good Book clearly shows that He was illegitimate. Either church folks should admit that Christ Himself shared in the wrong or they should stop slandering the ghetto mother. The only way for the current church attitude to be consistent with the Bible is to interpret the Christmas story this way: Illegitimacy is wrong, unless the illegitimate child ends up being the religious boss—the Son of God. You cannot bless one illegitimate birth and curse another one. The Apostle James said, "From the same mouth come blessing and cursing. My brethren, this ought not to be so." He was speaking to both church and society.

In America, we have a habit of cursing the underdog and branding the defenseless. The term "illegitimate child" is a contradiction. All children are the product of the same sexual act. The legitimate result of that sexual act is the birth of a child. The child born out of wedlock is the natural product of an illegitimate sexual act. Yet the statistics speak of "illegitimate children" and not "illegitimate mothers and fathers." We curse the underdog and brand the defenseless.

America's obsession with the Negro crime rate is another example of cursing the underdog and branding the defenseless. Billions of dollars made from dope, gambling, and prostitution are stolen from the greatness of America and all by white men. There are no Negroes in the Cosa Nostra. Just as there are very few Negro cops. At the time of the Watts riot, for example, there were fifty-one hundred cops in Los Angeles. Only 205 were Negro. And there were only four Negro cops in the 77th Precinct which is responsible for law enforcement in the Watts section of Los Angeles. In the history of the Los Angeles Police Department, a Negro had never been graduated above the rank of lieutenant.

When you speak of a Negro crime rate, you are really talking about a "Negro-arrested-by-the-police-and-convicted" rate! Go into any traffic court and you will see twice as many Negroes as whites. When I consider the population proportion, I refuse to believe that Negroes do twenty-eight times more speeding than white folks. America must ask herself the question: what would the white crime rate look like if the overwhelming majority of cops were Black Muslims?

"Relief" or "Foreign Aid"?

America curses the underdog on relief. "Relief" has become a dirty word in this country. An atmosphere has been created where people are ashamed to be on relief. If relief embarrasses or shames America, let it be called foreign aid. America is never embarrassed to send money all over Europe, for health projects and the like, and it is nothing but relief. A white man once asked me about the shame of the increasing number of colored folks on the relief rolls. I asked him, "Do you know any Africans on relief?" He answered, "No." So I said, "Then why didn't you leave us over there?"

I personally feel that all Negroes in this country should be on relief, regardless of their income. Relief is like my coming into your barn and stealing a horse. I put him in my stable. When the stolen horse gets hungry, I have to feed him. I would have to be a fool to come by your house and demand oats. Nor should the horse be expected to feed himself or be embarrassed that he is hungry. When a man decides to steal, he must accept the consequences of his theft. Relief is America paying her just dues for theft. It is the theft which is shameful, not the dues. I am tired of America balancing her wrongs by cursing my natural rights.

The irony is that the "curse" is really the "blessing." Having been on relief for twenty years, I have a personal resentment against it and wish that relief would be eliminated. Five minutes after my momma received her relief check, it was in the hands of that Right Wing bigot. He owned the business where Momma spent her money. Some seventeen million dollars a month is spent on relief in the state of Illinois. Though white folks curse relief, in all honesty the State of Illinois has to bless it. If relief were terminated, in ten months' time it would cost the State of Illinois $170 million. Knock that kind of revenue out of a state's economy and it is doomed.

When the State Kills

We speak of separation of church and state. I personally believe that the state has completely taken over the church. Even if you accept my momma's interpretation of "Thou shalt not kill" as covering only *human* life, the church is a long way from converting the state. The state is still allowed to kill the man who has killed. We still allow capital punishment in America. But two wrongs do not make a right. Have you ever stopped to consider who leads the condemned man to the killer? The minister or the priest! The state has completely taken over the church and uses it as a moment of final comfort for those whom the state would kill. I have often wondered what the clergyman says to the condemned man at the last moment before the execution. "Is there anything more I can do for you, son?" I would tell him, "Yes, Father. Stand here next to the electric chair and hold my hand." My Baptist preacher was always putting his foot in his mouth. I can just hear him saying to the condemned man as they are strapping him into the electric chair, "Well, son, this is as far as I go. I really don't know what to say, but more power to you."

Capital punishment is a disgrace. For the church to allow it to continue is an even greater disgrace. It is wrong for the church to tell me I should not kill and still be unwilling to make the same demand of the state. The greatest contradiction of all is for the clergyman to be present at the hour of the state's vengeance. If that same clergyman would go all the way and jump into the electric chair just once, it would end capital punishment immediately. Such an act would be a "sit-in" to end killing.

One of the most sacred acts of a Christian society is the act of marriage. Yet it is possible to bypass the church completely and get married by city hall. If you do go to the church to get married, you had better get things straight with city hall first.

A friend of mine was getting married and I was to be the best man. When we got to city hall, the old Justice of the Peace was sitting in his office surrounded by all those soldiers with their pregnant girls. And he was tired of it all. When my friend, his bride, and I walked into the office, the Justice never even looked up. He just mumbled his formalities and ended up with, "I now pronounce you man and wife." Then he looked up for the first time and told *me* to kiss the bride. That is how sacred marriage is in society today.

I cannot help but question how anything as sacred as marriage can depend upon the payment of a ten-dollar fee. If you went to city hall, got married, kissed your bride, and then told the Justice, "I'm not paying you," he probably would say, "Then it doesn't count." And you would not be married. Marriage has become that automatic and commercial and yet people wonder about the breakdown of the family.

President Johnson, backed by the statistics and findings of the Moynihan Report, has said that a breakdown of the family is responsible for the plight of the Negro in America. He is absolutely correct. America is my momma. And my momma was America to me. Since the United States Constitution is the farthest thing from the Negro in America, it is the last thing to be blamed for his plight. State, city, and county governments are closer, but they are still distant. My momma, as head of the family, was the only authority my America allowed me to touch. When my momma stole food from white folks, and justified it as necessary for survival, I did not blame the system. I did not blame a country where the black man is denied his constitutional rights; where Momma was stripped of her womanhood and Daddy of his manhood. I blamed Momma for stealing.

We got on the bus or streetcar and Momma always put my age back. The only thing a poor ghetto kid has is his God-given birthday. I was robbed of that. As Momma was robbed of her womanhood and Daddy of his manhood, I was robbed of my childhood. As a child, I didn't blame the system; I blamed Momma.

America Was Momma's Momma

Now that I am a man, I have "given up childish ways." I realize that America is my momma and America was Momma's momma. And I am going to place the blame for injustice and wrong on the right momma. Even today, when I leave my country to appear on television and make other public appearances in foreign countries, I find it difficult to speak of the injustices I experience in this country. Because America is my momma. Even if Momma is a whore, she is still Momma. Many times I am asked if I would go to war if drafted. I always answer, "Yes, under one condition; that I be allowed to go to the front line without a gun. Momma is worth dying for, but there is nothing worth killing for. And if I ever change my opinion about killing, I will go to Mississippi and kill that sheriff who spit in my wife's face."

America is my momma. One Fourth of July, I want to go to the New York harbor and talk to Momma—the Statue of Liberty. I want to snatch that torch out of her hand and take her with me to the ghetto and sit her down on the street corner. I want to show her the "tired, the poor, the huddled masses yearning to breathe free." I want to show Momma what she has been doing to her children. And Momma should weep. For the grief of the ghetto is the grief of the entire American family.

III

You have been told, O man, what is good,
And what the Lord requires of you:
Only to do justice, and to love kindness,
And to walk humbly with your God.

MICAH 6:8

Equal and exact Justice to all men of whatever state or persuasion, freedom of person under the protection of the Habeus Corpus, and trial by juries impartially selected: these principles form the bright constellation which has gone before us, and guided our steps through an age of revolution and reformation.

THOMAS JEFFERSON, March 4, 1801

WHO'S THE NIGGER TODAY?

When she was only four years old, my little daughter was marching in Birmingham, Alabama. In the process of demonstrating, she was hit in the eye with tear gas. About a year later we were talking about the experience, and my daughter surprised me by saying, "Daddy, I'll always *love* Sheriff Bull Conner, but I can never *respect* him."

What frightens me most about folks in the church is that they seem to think love and respect are the same thing. This confusion is the primary reason for the failure of the church the world over. When I say the church has failed, I am not speaking of the racial problem alone. There are churches in countries where there is no racial problem. And still the church has failed to make the gospel of love a working reality.

Love is an emotion, a passion which changes from time to time. You can love today and kill what you love tomorrow. A man and woman get married because they say they are in love. After a few months of married life they start fighting, and either one of them ends up dead or both end up in divorce court. Love changes. But respect is like good manners; it is constant. It governs a man's actions in every situation. The town drunk may never know a sober moment in his life. Yet he will not drink in front of his momma because he has too much respect for her.

You hear people say so often, "You can't legislate love." Until recently, nineteen states in America had laws on the books saying Negroes could not marry whites. If love is the true basis of marriage, such a law is legislating love. But there is a difference between love and respect. The law may not be able to require a man to love me, but it can require that he respect my human dignity.

Praying Over Stolen Food

I came from a family where I was expected to go to church on Sunday. I used to sit next to so many people who *loved* God—until the chips were down. My momma was like that. She was so busy loving God that it never occurred to her to respect Him. If she had respected God and the Bible, things would have been different in our house. Momma used to bring home food which she stole from the pantry of the white folks she was working for. She would cook it, serve it, and then *demand* that we pray over it. One day I took Momma down into the basement where I hid the things I had stolen. I said, "Here, Momma. You pray over what I have stolen and then I'll go back to the table and pray over what you have stolen." Momma didn't know that I was a better thief than she was. I just couldn't justify mine.

Then one day, when I was in my teens, I got caught snatching a pocketbook. I came back to my religious home and told Momma what had happened. She went to the white folks and got a lawyer. The next day in court, my momma sat and watched me put my hand on that Bible which she said she loved. She heard me solemnly swear to tell "the truth, the whole truth, and nothing but the truth, so help me God." For the next two hours she listened to me lie to beat the case. And when that judge said, "Not guilty," my momma jumped up and shouted, "Thank God!" If that isn't using the Creator to justify stealing, I don't know what is.

So there is a difference between love and respect. Every white man in the South has always had a Negro whom he loved. But he didn't respect one enough to go to the same toilet with him and that is the least common denominator of human activity.

The Half-Truth Hang-Up

Love is based on emotion and respect is based on justice. The problem comes when people talk about respect for law and order and try to bypass justice. In America, we are very good at developing cute little slogans based on half-truths. A popular slogan these days is "Equal opportunity means equal responsibility." That concept sounds good to sophisticated Negroes and educated white folks. But it doesn't make sense to the poor man in the ghetto. He knows it means that he is living in a country which is willing to give him 20 percent of his rights and is going to demand 400 percent responsibility in return. No matter what he does, the man in the ghetto gives back more responsibility than he gets rights.

If the degree of responsibility expected of a man is measured by the amount of opportunity open to him, there should be rioting every day in the ghetto. There is no real opportunity for the man in the ghetto; therefore responsibility has no meaning for him. The man in the ghetto cannot own a home; he has little chance of owning his own business; his schools are inferior and his employment opportunities are limited. Why should he be responsible? What America really means by the slogan "Equal opportunity means equal responsibility" is "Behave yourself and we may give you some opportunities."

Another popular phrase urges Negroes to "pick themselves up by their own bootstraps." I tried that when I was in the Army. If you really want to have some fun, try it yourself. Unlace your boots and just leave the lace in the bottom. Then give the lace a good jerk and your feet are going to come out from under you. All "lift yourself by your own bootstraps" means is that all colored folks will end up on their rumps. And perhaps white America is clever enough to realize that truth.

Respect for law and order is another phrase which doesn't sound right to the man in the ghetto. Look through the United States Constitution and the Bible and you will find that neither document is concerned with law and order. They both talk about justice. Somehow those old knicker-wearing cats who inked the Constitution knew that if you give a man 99.9 percent justice, he will give you law and order in return. But if you ask a man for law and order without placing him in a climate of justice, it is like asking him to breathe and placing him in a vacuum without any air, or telling him to bleed without giving him any blood.

Everything Nature demands of you, she gives you in advance. Then, if you violate her natural laws, you are in trouble. It is natural to expect men to live in peace and harmony within a climate of justice. Those who violate the law and order of an atmosphere of justice should be in trouble. But if this country is going to demand law and order before creating a climate of justice, it is going to have to hire one cop for every Negro in America and another cop for every white man. Such one-to-one policing sounds unnatural. But it is no more unnatural than demanding law and order while condoning the absence of justice.

America must learn that you can *postpone* justice, but you cannot *prevent* it. And the longer the postponement, the stiffer the penalty. For example, if I snatch your wallet tonight and get away, I am postponing justice. If I had been caught, I might have been sentenced to six months in jail. Since I got away, perhaps next week I will snatch your wallet again. If I get away, I am still postponing justice. Next year I may go for bigger stakes and, in the process, shoot and kill you. This time I am caught and sentenced to the electric chair. I have gone from an earlier six months' maximum to the death penalty. The longer you postpone justice, the stiffer the penalty.

Cleaning Up After the Party

America has been postponing justice so long that even the law-enforcement officer is now being treated unjustly. The same power structure which has been misusing the Negro for hundreds of years is now doing the same thing to the cop. The cop has become the new nigger in America. When I was a kid, my momma was America's nigger. She would go to work for white folks and couldn't come home until their party was over. She had to stay and clean up. Today, all over America, we go out and demonstrate for our rights. And the cop has to stay until our demonstration is finished. The difference is, Momma had a dust mop and a tea towel to perform her duties as a nigger. The cop has a badge and a gun. In many instances, the cop uses his badge and gun to break up the party. When Momma was the nigger, she could never do that with her dust mop. But someone still has to clean up the mess this cop is making. That is what I mean by calling the cop America's new nigger.

Now that it is the cop's turn to be the nigger, I can understand his reactions. They are the same as Momma's. When the Negro was America's nigger, he would take out his resentment in the white folks' pantry. Momma would come home every night with a shopping bag full of goodies. Raiding the pantry was her way of getting revenge for the injustices she had experienced. Today's cop, who is also the victim of injustice, relieves his resentment in the ghetto. As a nigger, the cop has to strike out against something. So he uses his nightstick on the head of the poor man in the ghetto. Every nigger has to have a pantry in which to relieve his resentment and frustration. And the head of the man in the ghetto is the cop's pantry. Is it any wonder that cops do not want a Civilian Review Board?

When my momma was the nigger she could never have taken a lie detector test in the white folks' bedroom and given an honest answer as to what happened to all the missing sheets. She would argue and ask if they didn't trust her. She would eventually convince her employers that the sheets were mislaid. In the same way, the cop can convince a whole society that he is not really being brutal in the ghetto. His attempt to rationalize and justify is not his fault, any more than it was my momma's fault. I did not like my momma stealing and I don't like what the cops are doing in the ghetto. But when cops become the victim of the same unjust system that has been victimizing Negroes all these years, the reaction will be the same for both cop and Negro.

I know it is hard for white folks to understand police brutality. They think Negroes are lying and creating a false issue. But when twenty-two million black folks start telling the same lie, white America had better start listening. If the average white man could darken his face and come into the ghetto, he would see what we are talking about firsthand.

When the cop is in a white neighborhood, he behaves like the public servant he is. We Negroes know this because we have seen it. We have worked in white folks' homes all our lives. When the cop comes into Miss Ann's house, the hat comes off and he is polite and courteous. He says "Mr." and "Mrs." and he has a search warrant. When that same cop comes into the ghetto apartment, he acts like a heathen in a foreign country. The hat stays on and courtesy goes out the window. The cop doesn't bother to get a warrant to search the ghetto apartment.

Police brutality penetrates deeper than the ultimate expression of the cop hitting me on the head. Police brutality is the brutal disrespect reflected in the cop's attitude when he is writing out my ticket. It is an attitude which allows the cop to call me "nigger" and "boy" and my woman "gal" when he is making an arrest.

There are Negroes in Chicago who hate to drive down the street seated next to a light-complexioned Negro woman, because the cop will think she is white. Because of this false assumption, the Negro man will be subjected to undue harassment. How long can a group of people endure such conditions of injustice before they react?

The Image Forced Upon the Cop

The absence of justice leads to disrespect and a breakdown of law and order. The cop shows disrespect for the residents of the ghetto as a reaction against the unjust conditions imposed upon him. It is unjust for society to send a cop into a trouble spot to solve this social problem he did not create. Nor is the cop adequately trained to actually solve the problem. The best he can do is try to suppress and contain it. But that makes about as much sense as sending in police to beat up cancer or polio. The only way to solve the problem of cancer or polio is to apply qualified minds to the task of basic research. If anything, the great social revolution in America demands more social workers and not more cops. When a cop arrives on the scene of trouble and strife, he so often shows by his behavior that he is mad at a situation which he is expected to solve, but which he did not create.

And the man in the ghetto shows disrespect for the cop as a reaction against his own personal unjust condition of poverty. This is unfortunate, because that cop who is out there beating heads with his nightstick is the same man who will go down in the sewer and rescue four little kids who are trapped. But the cop bears the image of the poverty enforcer. Society has forced this negative image upon him. The cop is as close as the man in the ghetto can get to the system which oppresses him. A close analogy can be drawn from earlier days of American history. The British soldier was not George Washington's real problem. The real enemies were the mother country and the man on the throne. But what the Redcoat represented to the American Revolution the Bluecoat represents to the revolution in the ghetto.

How can society ask a man to have respect for law and order when society itself does not have enough respect to treat the law-enforcement officer justly? Society gives its nigger, the cop, less rights than it gives the Negro. The Negro has the constitutional right to demonstrate his just grievances. But the cop better not be caught demonstrating! Society frowns on the cop demonstrating for a salary increase, for example, even though his pay is bad. When top-level politicians want a salary increase they have no difficulty getting it. Salaries are determined behind the closed doors of budget meetings. The cop cannot determine his salary in a secret meeting in the precinct house.

Since he is underpaid, the cop sometimes resorts to cheating. We have all read stories of cops looting stores and reporting burglaries. It is not an uncommon practice for cops to accept bribes. When the cop is caught cheating, he is subject to the same abuse in the newspapers as the poor man on relief. Everyone in town will be talking about the police scandal. When the millionaire is caught embezzling from the bank, society does not scandalize him. Such is society's disrespect for the cop.

City government uses the cop like a nigger. If the mayor receives a threatening telephone call, he calls a cop. And the cop will stand guard at the mayor's mansion around the clock. But the cop's life is threatened every day and he cannot call the mayor. If the cop arrests the "wrong" person, as politely as he can, there are repercussions from city hall. We had a cop in Chicago who had a habit of ticketing the "wrong" cars—cars belonging to prominent people. As a result, he was assigned to a safe, quiet, and secluded neighborhood where he spends his working hours guarding a drugstore. This is what happens to a cop who is bugging someone other than poor people!

Society cannot ask a man to have respect for law and order if the law itself does not have the same respect. The ghetto brother knows how many narcotics are sold in New York City every day. And he knows that the syndicate has to have the help of the police department to keep the narcotics traffic in operation. It is a common sight in the ghetto for the cop to turn his back as the junkies and pushers walk by or to see him smile at the pimps and the whores. Negroes who play policy every day have never seen the cop arrest the guy they know is carrying the drawings. The ghetto brother knows that part of his daily investment in the numbers racket goes to pay off the cop. Of course there is a reaction against the police department.

Such corrupt conditions endanger both the image and the life of the cop on the beat. As long as he can be questioned by the man in the street, the cop is in trouble.

He needs that man's respect to survive. In areas where there is a high rate of policemen killed, you will find a high syndicate crime rate and a tremendous degree of graft in the police department. A man does not kill what he respects. But when cops engage in activities which breed disrespect, their lives are in danger.

The civil rights movement has created new problems for the cop. One of the first lessons life in the ghetto teaches you is: "The rich man never gets the electric chair." The northern ghetto brother has been brutalized by the police for years. Such brutality was accepted as a normal fact of ghetto life. Yet the ghetto dweller has always noticed the difference in the manner in which the police dealt with the man who is well off.

A few years ago, television news reports started coming in from southern civil rights demonstrations. Northern white folks were shocked to see Sheriff Bull Conner turn the dogs on demonstrators in Birmingham, Alabama. The entire nation was upset to see open brutality on southern streets. But the man in the ghetto was not shocked. He has been subjected to the same mishandling all of his life. When he was shoved off the street corner for no reason, when his head received a brutal clubbing, and when dogs were used to terrorize him into compliance with the whim of the cop, there was no national reaction. Television cameras never focused upon these injustices. Suffering under a system of police oppression has always been simply a part of being black and living in a northern ghetto.

When the northern Negro saw the television coverage of southern civil rights demonstrations, and heard the reaction of an outraged nation, he suddenly became aware of his own constitutional rights. He began to ask questions about things he had never questioned before. The northern Negro living in the ghetto just did not know that a cop was not allowed to kick down his door and search his apartment without a warrant. He was not aware of his constitutional rights. But when he saw his southern brother raising the question of constitutional rights, the northern Negro began to ask why search warrants were not used in the ghetto. Southern demonstrations raised the question of the right of every citizen to walk down an American street without being harassed by the police. All of his life the northern ghetto brother has been stopped by a cop after dark and asked where he was going. He never questioned this practice before the southern demonstrations.

The demonstrations in the South made every Negro in America civil rights conscious. Because of this, northern cops could no longer engage in brutal activities without being questioned and challenged. Since the Bull Conner demonstrations, an increasing number of lawsuits have been filed against northern police departments. People who have been bitten by police dogs in the North, not because they were demonstrating but as a result of routine police practices, have been taking their cases to court. And private citizens are winning those cases.

The Cop and the Fireman

It is the fireman, not the cop, who comes the closest to treating society equally and showing the attitude of respect for all men which a climate of justice requires. The fireman operates on a higher level of intellect and understanding, either consciously or unconsciously. He is never mad at the fire when he arrives at your house to put it out. He knows that he did not start the fire. He cannot fight the fire destroying the ghetto home any slower than the fire in the rich man's mansion. Perhaps his attitude is different because he is fighting an abstract—fire.

If I am a cop and my partner is killed trying to apprehend a robber, I can take revenge on the next robber I am chasing. But if I am a fireman and the floor of a building collapses and kills my partner while we are fighting a fire, there is no direct revenge I can get at the next fire. The best I can do is learn from the accident and try to fight the next fire a little better.

The fireman views his job honestly and objectively. Have you ever heard a fireman being interviewed during a forest fire? He will say, "If we don't get a shift in the wind, we can't save the forest." It is the same with the social dilemma we are in today. If we don't get a shift in the wind, we won't be able to solve it. And there has been a shift in the wind in the ghetto, where the fireman had always been respected. During the demonstrations in 1963 in Birmingham, Alabama, fire hoses were turned on civil rights demonstrators. Yet not one northern fireman raised his voice in protest. As a result, the fireman now bears the same false image in the ghetto which society has inflicted upon the cop. The power structure cannot expect to solve the social problems of the ghetto by the mere physical presence of cops. The violence and strife in the ghetto cannot be contained or suppressed because they do not represent a riot. Five disciplined cops can stop a riot, but the best trained armies in the world cannot contain a legitimate protest.

The attitude of the cop is much more important than his physical presence. If you live in a city whose baseball team has just won the World Series, or which has been chosen by the Shriners as the site for their national convention, you will see people take over the town. They get drunk in the streets, damage property, and bother passersby. The cop will look the other way because a big convention is bringing the city millions of dollars. If a cop can be taught to change his attitude because a convention is bringing a city a lot of money, he had also better be taught not to mistreat people who are demanding human dignity, which is more than all the money in the world can buy.

People insist that it is unfair to generalize about the police. The good cop is held up for public inspection and he is supposed to be the example of law-enforcement officers everywhere. Just as the one rabbi, priest or minister who goes to Alabama to demonstrate is supposed to represent the whole church. The one beautiful cop in a neighborhood *will* stand out. He has pride in his job. He is sensitive to human problems and knows how to talk to the person on the street corner. He has not chosen his job because he couldn't get hired any place else. He is a cop because he wants to be; perhaps his father and grandfather before him had devoted their lives to law enforcement.

The problem cops, and there are many, are those who resented their job when they took it. They are the cops who act like the judge and the jury when they make an arrest. Their resentment shows twenty-four hours a day. This situation will never change until society gives law enforcement a status which is comparable to the job it is expected to do.

Give the Cop His Due

Policemen labor under two basic injustices: inadequate salary and lack of proper training. The cop is the most underpaid man in American society today. Cops in the large cities should begin with a minimum salary of ten thousand dollars per year. You must pay a proper dollar for the job required. More and more potential teachers are lost to the vocation of education because industry is able to pay more money. The cop is so important to solving the social problems which beset the ghetto that America should take the chance of overpaying him, not underpaying him.

Being an entertainer, I am constantly reminded of the financial injustice which the cop suffers. I have done benefit performances all over the country for Policemen's Wives, Policemen's Widows, Policemen's Benevolence Associations, and so on. But I never did a show for the politician's wife or the nightclub owner's wife. They are able to provide for their family in case of emergency, because their earnings are at a higher level than the cop's. If America treated the cop with the respect his job deserves, the family of a cop killed in the line of duty would automatically become the responsibility of government. Some local governments have accepted this responsibility, but such legislation should be enacted across the country in a uniform way.

Imagine yourself a cop in a major urban area. When you put on that uniform in the morning and leave the house, you never know if you will make it back home in the evening. The policeman must live daily with a basic human fright which few other professions share. Yet the cop pays the same price for his haircut that Rockefeller pays. He pays the same amount for the education of his children that the rich executive pays. If a policeman is killed in the line of duty, it is an ethical and moral imperative that society accept the responsibility of scholarships for his children, a home for his family, and other necessary benefits.

Somehow we seem to be able to give foreign aid to countries all over the world, even those countries who openly tell us to "go to hell." We should be able to find the money to give some aid to the cop—proper salary and proper training. Domestic aid to the cop at home is more important than foreign aid to countries abroad. We have a crisis in this country which can destroy us from within. People talk about Nero fiddling while Rome burned. LBJ is fiddling while the ghettos of this nation burn. The number one place to begin to solve this problem which calls attention to itself with the haunting chant, "Burn, baby, burn," is through enlightened law enforcement.

There is a psychological factor operating in the injustice to the cop. A man knows when he is being mistreated and it is bound to affect his attitude. This applies to both Negroes and cops. When we finally create an atmosphere in this country where law-enforcement officers are trained and paid in direct proportion to the importance of their job, a new attitude of vocational pride will be evident. If society does not have enough pride in its law-enforcement officers to pay them what they are worth, the cop is more likely to be susceptible to the bribe. If the pay scale is high enough, the cop does not want to risk getting caught taking a bribe for fear of losing his job. He knows he cannot get another job at the same high salary. Honesty and devotion are basic ingredients in vocational pride.

There is also the consideration of security, which is especially important in a dangerous profession. The soldier has security, although often he is not even aware of it. Count up his benefits and you will find that he has much more security than the cop. And the soldier's job is easier than the cop's, because the soldier knows where his enemy is. The enemy even wears a uniform to identify himself. But the cop doesn't know what his enemy looks like. It might be that nut the Army rejected! The same man who is too crazy to go to Vietnam and kill Vietcong is back home in your neighborhood waiting to assault you. The cop has to deal with him.

Each new technological advance and the prospect of life in a cybernetic society will place more demands upon the cop. We will see unions demanding shorter and shorter work weeks. There will be an increase of leisure time. People will have more time on their hands, perhaps to be out in the streets. When a man works a forty-hour week, the cop can count on the foreman watching him at least eight hours a day!

The prophet Micah insisted that the Lord requires simply that man "do justice." He seems to imply that other problems of human relationship will be solved when a climate of justice is established. Justice in America today requires the investment of funds for the proper training and schooling of law-enforcement officers. The cop's job is too important for him to be allowed to put on the uniform without proper training. When I travel to England, it is frightening to see that the cabdriver in London receives a longer period of training than the average cop in America. Surely we must see our cops as more crucial to the total health of society than England does its cabdrivers. Only through basic research and proper training can just and enlightened law enforcement become a reality. And this enlightenment and sensitivity must come *before* the cop gets out into the street. Society simply cannot send the cop out into the street with his nightstick to get on-the-job training on my head or with my problems, which he has not been trained to understand. He must become thoroughly aware of my social problems while he is still in school. All the force in the world will never totally suppress a legitimate problem. Those who would deal with social problems must have a basic human understanding.

The cop must be taught the unique problems of ghetto living *before* he ever goes out on his beat. He must know, for example, why the man in the ghetto rarely shops at the supermarket. The supermarket requires him to pay cash. So the man in the ghetto goes to the white local merchant across the street. The prices in that little store are too high already, and the local merchant will try to cheat even more. The ghetto brother knows he is being cheated and it worries him. So when the white merchant turns his back to get the stale day-old loaf of bread, his customer wipes out the cookie rack. It is the customer's way of making up for the cheat. While the merchant is busy putting his thumb on the scale, his pickles disappear.

The cop must understand this injustice. He will see that there is more to the issue than a customer stealing. But if the customer gets caught stealing, the merchant calls a cop. When the ghetto kid gets caught stealing, the merchant grabs him by the ears and holds him until the cops arrive. But what happens when that same kid gets shortchanged by the merchant? The kid can't call a cop and get a fair hearing. Cops must be taught to have a responsive and sympathetic ear and listen when that ghetto mother complains that her kids are being shortchanged. Once a cop becomes aware of such practices from the beginning, he can go immediately to the local merchant and say, "We have tremendously explosive social problems in this neighborhood which you could tip off at any moment. Don't shortchange the kids." And if complaints continue to come in, the cop should investigate the basis of the complaint immediately. Such activity would go a long way toward establishing a new image of respect for the cop in the ghetto. And the resentment and frustration which lead to breaking the local merchant's window and looting his store would begin to be alleviated.

The Cop and the Ghetto Kid

Understanding ghetto kids presents a special problem for the cop. When a riot breaks out in a high school, the damage is already done and there is little the cop can do besides try to contain the violence. But if the cop had been sensitive to the history of the problem, the riot might have been avoided. For example, two kids have a gun duel in the schoolyard. The incident will very probably be hushed up by the school principal to keep his own record clean downtown. He doesn't want the superintendent of schools questioning his ability to control his pupils. But the seed for further trouble has been sown. A full-scale school riot may erupt which is certainly a more destructive mark on the principal's record.

Cops need to learn to work hand in hand with the school. They need to learn to meet ghetto kids on their own level—the "'cause why" level. It is that basic, raw, instinctive level of life which seeks honest and open answers to very basic questions. High school kids know that the cops will be on hand when they throw their dance. 'Cause why is that the only time the cops are around? The cop has the image of only coming around to break up a party.

When cops learn to meet kids on their own level, they will learn the answer to many adolescent mysteries. Like why so many kids choose the street corner or the local hangout instead of the brand-new recreational facilities in the neighborhood. It is a simple fact of nature. Recreational facilities are geared to a program for boys. But the boys are going to choose to be where the girls are. The girls are at the local hangout. There are certain biological factors which take precedence even over basketball!

When cops learn the conditions of the home environment in the ghetto, they will find out why kids act as they do. How many cops on the beat have actually seen their mother have an affair with their own daddy, let alone another man. Or how many cops have seen their mother take a needle and stick it in her arm and get high? The ghetto kid has seen this. He has looked at his own mother have an affair with a stranger. Of course, she told him it was one of Daddy's friends who came by to talk to her. So they went into the bedroom to talk, closing the door behind them. But Mother never thought that her little seven-year-old kid would peek through the keyhole. After he peeked through the keyhole and saw what he saw, he came back out into the street. He has just seen his mother have an affair with a stranger and the cop is going to tell him to be good? Naturally he will start swinging on the cop because he has to react against something. He can't swing on Momma.

The cop has to go back home with the ghetto kid and find out where he learned that language he uses. Mother and Father would never curse in front of the kid, until they get angry. Then the curse words fly. When you hear these words at age seven, you assume that a dirty word is something to be used as a defensive weapon. So when you walk down the street and a little girl says to you, "You stink," quite naturally you are angry and threatened. It is only natural to turn and say, "Kiss my butt." It is natural because the little seven-year-old has heard Mother and Father use dirty language under the same threatening conditions. The little kid doesn't take a bite out of a good piece of chicken and curse. He smacks his lips and makes funny little grunting noises, just like Momma and Daddy. But when he is threatened, angry, and misused, the little kid curses. His home environment has taught him that response.

Cops must be trained to understand, on the human level, the conditions of life and the home environment. It is amazing to see the results of juvenile police who have received private grants to work with kids. They accept the gang leader and work with him. They do not start out resenting him and trying to force him to behave. A loyalty is established between cop and gang, so that the cops often know when and where the big rumble is going to be. By really becoming involved in the life of the gang, and accepting kids on their own level, juvenile cops have been able to contain potentially troublesome situations.

Just and proper training of cops must take into account the tremendous responsibility placed upon law-enforcement officers and the great pressures under which they live. Can you imagine a cop running through the streets of New York City, chasing a burglar, and he shoots, missing the culprit and hitting the Russian diplomat coming out of the United Nations Building? That is World War Three! Such is the awesome responsibility placed upon the man with the gun.

Imagine the mental pressure a cop must live under daily in the ordinary line of duty. He sees daily the horror we only read about in the newspapers. We read about a three-year-old girl being sexually molested, mutilated, and murdered. The cop sees it for himself. He walks into an apartment minutes after a man has gone berserk and chopped up his wife and mutilated his kids. Perhaps the cop has little kids of his own waiting for him to come home. What does such a gruesome sight do to a man's mind? How does it affect a man mentally to daily smell and touch dead human beings? It is the cop's job to live in an atmosphere of death—to see dead kids, to hear people moaning, groaning, and crying for help. Society expects the cop to experience such sickening horror and to take it in his stride. He is expected to forget what he has seen and walk back out on the street without holding a grudge. Have we done enough basic research to find out what such an occupational atmosphere does to a cop, as a man? Without such basic research, he cannot be adequately trained to deal with the conditions which his job impose upon him. The cop's daily work is certain to affect him mentally. One cannot witness daily the horrible reminders of the worst that man can do without developing a low evaluation of humanity. Just and proper training for the cop must take this inevitable reaction into account.

Respect for law and order can never be expected until a climate of justice is created which encompasses both the cop and the man in the ghetto. The cop has to be an authority before he gets into the neighborhood. He must be trained to be an expert in understanding human behavior. He must be skilled in the art of human relationships. He must be a general practitioner trained to doctor social ills. If the cop is not adequately trained, he may be doing the very best he can given the conditions of his job; but his best is still wrong. A man does not become a brain surgeon by receiving on-the-job training in the emergency room of a hospital. The surgeon receives basic knowledge and training in medical school. Then he is ready to operate on a cracked skull and see the raw horror of an exposed brain. He will become a better surgeon with each new operation. But he is trained for his task before he is allowed to perform his very first operation. Basic knowledge and training precede actual practice. And the same thing must happen with law enforcement.

If the man on the street is to respect law and order, the cop must behave like a trained, enlightened authority. A man does not want his authority getting angry, swinging a nightstick, and cursing. Such behavior is like the brain surgeon panicking at the sight of a skull fracture after an automobile accident. If that happens, you might just as well close down the hospital. The patient will die when he sees the look of horror on the surgeon's face. The surgeon is expected to take the crisis in his stride and do his job.

It is the same with the cop. It is easy for the cop to walk down the street when nothing is going on, beating his stick on the lamppost and waving with a friendly word for everyone sitting on the tenement stoop. But can the cop keep this same air of cool, calm, and authority in the midst of crisis?

Reacting to Birth Pangs

Almost every day a cop performs duties as a matter of routine which would scare me to death. A woman giving birth to a baby in the back seat of my car, for example. It doesn't scare the average cop because he has been trained to know what to do when that water bag bursts before the woman gets to the hospital. He recognizes that it is an act of Nature and he knows how to deal with it.

The social revolution in the sore spots of this nation is another act of Nature, a natural response to oppressive conditions. It bears the same marks of pain, violence, and struggle which accompany any birth. From this violent, painful struggle a new America will be born. For the first time, the nation will be christened in the name of freedom, dignity, and justice. During this transitory period of pregnancy, justice demands that the cop be trained to display the same authority and sophistication in the midst of social crisis as he does when a woman gives birth to a baby in the back of his patrol wagon.

It has been said, "Justice belongs to all men, or it belongs to none." Aristotle wrote, "The way to gain good will is to show good will." And the prophet Micah reminds us what the Lord requires for men to live together in peace, love, and harmony, "do justice, love kindness and walk humbly with your God." What better description could there be for a climate in which respect for law and order is guaranteed? To *do* justice means to treat all men with respect and human dignity—Negroes, whites, cops, and all of creation. To love kindness is to consciously seek an atmosphere of human dwelling in which the rights and needs of all men are respected. To walk humbly means to maintain an air of sensitivity which seeks first to understand human expression rather than to thwart or suppress it. Such is the climate of justice. And when that climate is created, respect for law and order—even an increase of genuine love—will follow.

IV

Out of the depths have I cried unto thee, O Lord!
Lord, hear my voice!
Let thine ears be attentive to
The voice of my supplication.

PSALMS 130:1–2

Judge not, that you be not judged. For with the judgment you pronounce you will be judged, and the measure you give will be the measure you get. . . . You hypocrite, first take the log out of your own eye, and then you will see clearly to take the speck out of your brother's eye.

MATTHEW 7:1, 2 and 5

IF YOU CUT ME, I AM GOING TO BLEED

"Judge not, that you be not judged. For with the judgment you pronounce you will be judged, and the measure you give will be the measure you get." These words of Jesus are a sober reminder to America. America has been so busy judging the black ghetto that she has refused to be attentive to the voice of supplication crying out from the depths of ghetto life. As a result the judgment has turned upon America, and the measure of apathy and denial which she has given has been returned with chaos and disorder.

Nothing makes me more angry than to hear Negroes pass judgment on the black ghetto. A Negro doctor said to me one day, "Why do those people riot and tear up their own property? If they really want to accomplish something, they should tear up Saks Fifth Avenue." I gave him an honest, angry answer. I told him, "The ghetto brother is too brilliant to do your dirty work for you. You shop at Saks Fifth Avenue, but he doesn't. If you want your credit records burned up, you will have to do it yourself. The problem of the man in the ghetto is right in his own neighborhood and that is what he will burn up."

Destruction of one's own property is nothing new to American revolutions. When the Sons of Liberty dumped the tea in the water, they were destroying their own property. Great Britain did not send all that tea across the water on credit. What happened at the Boston Tea Party was not a protest against the problems of Boston. Rather, it was symbolic of the problem of oppression facing all the colonies. And Britain was as uninformed and stupid in handling her colonies as America is in handling the problem of the ghetto.

America has refused to listen to the brilliant, natural voice of the ghetto and has preferred to pass judgment instead. The words of Jesus ring out to America, "You hypocrite, first take the log out of your own eye, and then you will see clearly to take the speck out of your brother's eye." If America would observe the wounds she has inflicted in the ghetto, rather than judging the actions of the wounded, the social problem could be solved.

Any competent and trained sociologist from a foreign country could arrive in America knowing nothing of the problem of the Negro in this country. As soon as the sociologist drove through a black ghetto on his way home from the airport, he would immediately say, "There is an oppressor somewhere in this country." His eye is trained to recognize the human behavior which indicates the marks of oppression.

It is like a man who is wounded in an automobile accident. If he is lying on the street bleeding, it is folly to tell him not to bleed. A man cannot hide his wounds, for bleeding is Nature's way of telling where the wound is. When the ambulance arrives, the attendants look for the bleeding man so that they can rush him to the hospital for thorough treatment. It would be insanity for the ambulance attendants to pass judgment upon the man because he is bleeding and messing up the street. Sanity dictates that they recognize the serious nature of the wound and get emergency treatment as soon as possible.

Every Man Needs an Address

But America prefers to judge the bleeding rather than treat the wound. Giant new housing projects are constructed in the black ghettos of major cities and thousands of ghetto poor are crowded into them. Soon the voices of judgment are heard. They say, "Why don't those people appreciate these new buildings? They throw garbage, beer cans, and wine bottles out of the windows and the projects are not safe to walk through at night." Such judgment fails to recognize the bleeding indicating the wounds that new housing projects inflict upon their residents.

In a capitalistic system, every man needs an address. His own personal address is part of a man's identification as a unique individual citizen in this land. When the new housing projects are constructed, they are given a name rather than an address. The buildings are called the Taylor Homes in Chicago or the Fort Green Projects in Brooklyn, New York. Such naming robs a man who lives in the housing project of his individuality, because it deprives him of an address.

When I was a poor kid living in the ghetto of St. Louis, I had an address. If I snatched a pocketbook, my name and address appeared in the paper, "Dick Gregory, 1803 North Taylor." I was personally and individually identified as the thief. It was me, no doubt about it. But in the new housing project, where twelve thousand or more Negroes are living together, *everyone* has the same address. If one man walks out into the street and hits another man on the head, the story appears in the paper, "John Doe, Taylor Homes." Immediately, every other resident of Taylor Homes shares the guilt of the crime. The housing project takes the rap rather than the individual criminal himself. If a man has his own unique address, he is responsible for his own individual wrongdoing and his neighbors do not have to share the blame.

When enough stories appear in the newspaper indicting the entire housing project, the project develops a reputation. If you tell a man he is bad long enough and often enough, he will begin to believe it himself and will try to live up to that image. Consequently, when a stranger walks through the new housing project, someone will walk up to him and say, "Man, what are you doing here? Don't you know how bad we are in Taylor Homes? Just read the newspaper." And the stranger will be beaten or mugged because of that strange natural tendency of a man to feel compelled to live up to his reputation. Such is the bleeding which results from the wound of being deprived of an address.

The System Makes Him a Litterbug

Still the voices of judgment say, "Why are they not grateful for those new buildings? Why must they litter the courtyard and destroy the property?" Littering is a normal reaction to a system of oppression which deprives a man of the right of property ownership and places him in a new building which lacks the decent conveniences other people enjoy. If you depreciate a man's soul, he will react by depreciating your property. If you cut a man, it is only normal for him to bleed. The abnormality is cutting him in the first place. Littering is the bleeding wound of soul depreciation.

Those who enjoy the right of property ownership and build a house according to their own specifications include a recreation room in the basement. The playroom is the place to have fun, to raise hell, and not have to worry about destroying the wall-to-wall carpet in the living room.

In the recreation room, you do not worry about spilling beer on the linoleum.

The poor man in the ghetto housing projects does not enjoy the luxury and convenience of a recreation room. And the bedroom floor in his crowded apartment is as valuable to him as the rich man's wall-to-wall carpet. The project courtyard or the street corner is the only recreation room the poor man in the ghetto has. And it is where he does his littering.

The hypocrites who pronounce judgment upon littering in the ghetto would not complain if Negroes were cluttering the streets with diamonds or uranium. They would come by every day and sweep up the litter. Nor do the voices of judgment stop to consider why there are so many liquor and wine bottles in the ghetto with which to litter. Negroes in Chicago comprise a third of the total population, but they consume 65 percent of all the alcohol sold. Negroes consume over 90 percent of all the half-pints sold in Chicago. The crucial question is not why the littering, but rather why such a high rate of consumption of alcohol in ghetto neighborhoods? What is the man in the ghetto trying to forget? What forces of oppression drive him to seek mental relief through drinking?

All men react the same way to unbearable mental pressure and strain. The man in the ghetto lives every moment with the mental pressure of wondering how he is going to pay his bills, wondering when the rat is going to attack his babies, and tormenting himself with the thought that his children cannot get the proper education to escape ghetto life. With such mental pressure upon him, the man in the ghetto does not see grass growing nor does he respect property he does not own. The property is owned by the same system which oppresses him.

White folks react the same way under mental strain. If

the stock market fell for six successive weeks in America, rich white folks would be checking into downtown hotels and jumping out of nineteenth-floor windows. Committing suicide is littering property with your own body. I cannot imagine a worse form of littering. Yet the littering is directly related to unbearable mental pressure and Nature causes all men to react alike to such strain.

Doorbells and Relief

The voices of judgment complain of the growing number of Negroes on the relief rolls. One of the solutions to the problem is a simple matter of installing doorbells in the housing projects. Imagine you are a bill collector sent to make a collection in one of the new housing projects. Since there are no doorbells on the ground floor of the housing project, you must go up twenty stories to the individual apartment to find out if anyone is home. Most of the time the elevators are out of order, so you may have to walk. After you have walked up twenty flights of stairs, you discover that no one is home. If the same pattern continues with your next six customers, you return to your office without having made a single collection. You are tired and weary and do not want to go through the same process the next day. So you put a garnishee on your customer's salary.

Many states in America have laws saying that if a man gets behind in the payment of his debt to his creditors, the creditor is legally permitted to put a wage assignment on the man's salary the same as the Internal Revenue. Such a wage assignment, or garnishee, causes so much legal and book work for the employer that the man is automatically fired after two or three assignments, over a specified period of time.

The poor man in the ghetto is the last person in the

world who needs a garnishee on his salary. Once he is fired because of wage assignments, the man in the ghetto knows how difficult it is, as a Negro, to get another job. The fact that his salary has been assigned on the last job makes future employment even more difficult. Employers will refuse to take a chance hiring him. Knowing that his family must eat, and caring more for his family than he does for what white America thinks about relief, the man in the ghetto will take whatever steps are necessary to place his family on the relief rolls. To get his family on relief, he must move out of the housing project, so that his wife can enroll for support. A family is broken up and the relief rolls are increased, all because of a lack of doorbells.

Give the Kid a Toilet

Not only are there no addresses and no doorbells in the new housing project buildings, but there are also no public toilets. Yet people wonder why there is a strong smell of urine in the hallways and elevators of the brand-new buildings.

In downtown office buildings or department stores there are toilets on every floor. There are no children in those office buildings, only grown men who should be able to hold their water. Thousands of little children live in the housing projects. Yet there are no toilets except in the child's own apartment. When a little five-year-old kid goes outside to play, he is going to stay out until the last possible moment. He knows that Momma might make him stay in the apartment if he goes back upstairs.

So when Nature calls while that little kid is outside playing, he has to get on the slow elevator and go up twenty stories to respond to Nature's call. He doesn't pass a toilet on the way up, so naturally the elevator becomes his toilet. Is it any wonder that the elevators smell of urine? The downtown office buildings would have a strong aroma if there were no toilets and a slop jar under every desk. A little kid does not have to go up twenty stories in a department store, such as Macy's or Marshall Field, to find a toilet. The problem of the thousands of little kids living in the housing project would be solved simply by adding a public toilet on the ground floor or on every third floor.

Bigger Than a Head-Box

America has chosen to judge the voice of ghetto supplication rather than be attentive to it. The voice which speaks out of the depths of ghetto life is born of oppression and injustice and possesses an instinctive natural brilliance all its own. There is a network of communication and an instinctive understanding in the ghetto which is impossible to escape once you have lived there. Even Negroes who have become successful and moved out still have deep roots in the ghetto. The white man in America who makes five thousand dollars per year knows very few other white men who make ten thousand dollars a year and even fewer who make fifty or a hundred thousand dollars. Such is the social regimentation in the white community. Economic condition determines intimate social relationships. This is not true in the ghetto. Every poor Negro knows something about the Negro who has made it.

I made a million dollars in 1961 and 1962. I flew to Los Angeles and checked into a sixty-five-dollar-a-day room in the Beverly Hilton Hotel. Riding up to my room on the elevator, one of the ghetto sisters who was working as a maid turned to me and said, "How are you doing, baby?" Then she began to tell me about my daddy! Because of the segregated system that has forced all Negroes to live together, any Negro who is doing well knows that there is a mental file on him in any ghetto in the country.

It is Nature's way to compensate with instinct what the unnatural forces of oppression have denied by way of education. The tight system of oppression has produced a box in the head of every ghetto resident which tunes in to provide instant communication. The story of Rafer Johnson illustrates this unique communication. Rafer Johnson was one of the greatest athletes of all time. He was the Negro athlete who was the pride and joy of the black community. He set new world records in the decathlon and the Russians carried him off the track on their backs. Rafer Johnson was well educated and a symbol of black pride.

Rafer Johnson's name is seldom mentioned in the ghetto today. Why? Because Hollywood turned on that little box in the mind of every ghetto resident. When Rafer Johnson came back to America, the movie industry took off his Ivy League suit and his Phi Beta Kappa key and put him in an African movie with a spear in his hand. That little box told every ghetto brother to be ashamed.

When you shop at a supermarket, notice that you will seldom see a Negro woman put her black baby in a basket and ride him around. Nor will you see a Negro baby being led around by one of those leather leashes white mothers use to keep their children under control. Stores would be more than willing to sell leashes to a Negro mother and no one has ever told her not to use them. But that little box in her head tells the ghetto mother that there is so much hatred for a black baby in our society that she must hold him in her arms.

Natural Power

Nature also has a way of compensating to grant power to the powerless. The man in the ghetto has had a profound effect upon the stock market in this country, even though he is too poor to invest. Assume you are a white man who owns a supermarket in a Negro neighborhood. There have been no riots in your city but you have a latent fear that one might erupt at any moment. Your usual order for one item, Campbell Soup for example, is forty cases. By ordering such a quantity you get three cases free and are able to underprice the small store owner.

When the Campbell Soup salesman comes in to take your order while the fear of rioting is on your mind, you only order two cases. You do not want to have a large inventory on hand for the looters to grab. The Campbell Soup company is stuck with thirty-eight cases of soup which they had counted on selling. This is just one item in one store in one Negro neighborhood. Multiply that loss by hundreds of thousands of items in thousands of stores in hundreds of neighborhoods, and you will be able to compute the effect the fear of rioting has upon the stock market. If the company cannot move the product out of the warehouse, it must discontinue manufacturing.

If you own the Cadillac or Lincoln franchise in a neighborhood where rioting is feared as an immediate possibility, you will not stock up on excess automobiles. You will tell Detroit to keep their cars until conditions calm down at home. As a result, the national economy is seriously undermined. Such is Nature's way of granting power to the powerless.

White Man, Listen

Even those people who attempt to listen to the voice of ghetto supplication are not truly attentive. Welfare departments send social case workers into ghetto apartments to search for evidence of a man in the house to establish the validity of a family's right to be on relief. All the while they are searching for men's shoes under the bed or ties in the closet, little children are running around. Nature decrees that the presence of children indicates the prior presence of a man. Social workers should accept that normal fact of life and start conducting interviews rather than searching for evidence. Basic social research, based on an honest listening to the voice of the ghetto, is the only solution to America's problem.

When America becomes truly attentive to the supplicating voice of the black ghetto and removes the log of indifference and judgment from her own eye, she will be able to see clearly to remove the speck of suffering from the eye of the ghetto. Until relief from oppression is granted, the only appropriate name for America is "you hypocrite!"

V

Jesus said to them, "Render to Caesar the things that are Caesar's, and to God the things that are God's."

MARK 12:17

Everyone is talking about unidentified flying objects these days. A white minister told me the other day that he had been reading about UFO's and then he asked, "How come no colored folks have been seeing them?" I informed him, "We've been seeing them for seventy-five years and people called them ghosts." Personally, I am surprised that anyone has been seeing unidentified flying objects. I feel if any *intelligent* beings existed on another planet, they wouldn't come down here. Every time I hear a report of an unidentified flying object, it makes me wonder just how intelligent life on other planets can be. Intelligent and sensible life would have no part of man's actions toward his fellow man on this planet.

Life on this planet is so obsessed by that mad term "power." We seem to think that bombs and weapons are "power." But all over the South that myth has been exploded. When the Ku Klux Klan got out their bigot arsenal and started bombing and burning churches, those churches got fuller. All of a sudden, the Klan realized their little peashooters didn't scare anyone but themselves.

Any time a man can throw a bomb into a church window and not kill any more than three or four people, he had to be scared when he threw it. The people are sitting in church praying, with their eyes closed mind you, and only three or four are killed. The man had to be running when he threw the bomb! There is only one thing that can stop colored folks in America and even the Klan can't get their hands on that *big* bomb.

I was thinking the other day, wouldn't it be weird if we did get invaded from outer space? We would get out our whole arsenal and fight the invaders with nuclear bombs. But wouldn't it be wild if, after five days of fighting, we suddenly realized that atomic fallout was protein to creatures from outer space; that hand grenades, bullets, bombs, and cursing were like ice cream and cake to them; and the only way to destroy them would be through love and affection? We sure would lose that war!

Such an invasion from outer space would be a valuable lesson for man. He needs to have something from the outside jump on him and show him that his little pistol is no good any more. The only thing which can save man he was born with—love. Love is man's natural endowment, but he doesn't know how to use it. He refuses to recognize the power of love because of his love of power.

Man needs to learn how insignificant he really is in the total scheme of things. If he realized this, he would stop grasping for power. If every man on the face of the earth committed suicide, it would not affect the sun, the moon, or the stars. They would still have the same function. But if the sun committed suicide by crashing into the earth, all men would die. And man needs to learn the insignificance of the things he treasures. Man values money. Yet one man, a doctor, devotes his life to discovering a cure for polio. Perhaps he realizes $100,000 for his discovery. Another man hits a golf ball for two days and realizes $200,000 for his effort. Money is no measure of the worth of a man.

The continuing struggle for human dignity is instructing

the entire nation about the true measure of man's worth. When I was in Alabama in 1965, during the first election after the passage of the voting rights bill, I began to see the first fruits of that struggle. It was the first time I ever closed my eyes at night in the state of Alabama. Things had changed radically, not over a period of years, but in only a few months' time. And I know the activity in the South will produce more changes all over the country. That election demonstrated to me how the southern Negro is embarrassing both Negroes and whites in the North. This embarrassment was partially responsible for the Watts riot. Those Negroes were so mad at seeing their southern brother get all the goodies.

When the northern white man sees what is happening in the South, he is frightened and embarrassed because he knows he has been tricking northern Negroes so long. Northern white folks have been convincing us that we northern Negroes are better off than we would be down South. And we believed them. Then we look down and see those new southern voters talking about a Negro sheriff. How many northern towns have a colored sheriff? Or a colored police commissioner? Up North, colored folks can only run for office according to that old rule—that they allow white folks to tell them how to act after they are elected. We have always had some Negro politicians in office in the North. But before the civil rights bill was passed, you never heard many of them speak out on national television.

In the North, Negroes have always had the right to *elect*, but they have never had the right to *select*. Northern Negroes have never been allowed to decide who they want to represent them. They have only been allowed to vote after the candidate has been hand-picked by the white establishment. But now that same establishment is getting nervous. Northern politicians are seeing a southern Negro not only with voting power, but also with the freedom and independence to select his own candidate. Northern Negroes never made a white man scared enough to run home and get his wife to help him out. But that is what the Negroes of Alabama did to George Wallace. And if Wallace had been a bachelor, he probably would have run home and got his momma. No man is supposed to get that upset! There was a time when Negroes who were doing bad up North could look down on their southern brother and say, "At least, we're not doing as bad as they are in Alabama." But that isn't true any more.

Recently in Chicago, the Police Commissioner came out with a new order saying the police could no longer refer to Negroes as "niggers." A Chicago cop called me one night, "Come here, nigger." I looked at his partner and said, "Your man is calling you." I don't look or act like a nigger, so I don't get called that very often. I just thought this particular cop was out of line. I have been living in Chicago for ten years and did not realize that cops were actually allowed to call Negroes "niggers." And why did the new order come out in 1966? Because of what has been happening in the South.

For years civil rights demonstrators have been in the southern streets shattering the business and disturbing the peace through nonviolent marches, raising all kinds of cain to make our democracy work right. Now that we have a couple of civil rights bills, everyone wants to get sweet and sentimental about how it happened. But remember what was said and done when the demonstrations first started. Dogs were set loose and tear gas was used. The civil rights demonstrators learned to swallow it and come back for more. Of course, I could never understand why anyone would shoot tear gas at us. We have enough to cry about already.

Why Credit the Communists?

The same thing was said about demonstrations in the South that is now being said about riots in the North. "They are Communist-inspired." I am so sick and tired of the Communists getting credit for all of the good things we do. They never get blamed for bad things. Nobody ever gives the Communists credit for the dope traffic in this country or sees them infiltrating prostitution rings.

The boys in Washington will not even give black folks in this country credit for being legitimately mad on their own. They say a pattern of internal disorder is what the Communists are trying to create. The pattern is supposed to prove Communist infiltration. If J. Edgar Hoover, the head of the country's top security, can make a blanket accusation about Communists in the civil rights movement and not give their names, he is giving the Communists more protection than he is giving us.

Then you hear it said that Communists have not taken over the civil rights movement, but a small percentage has infiltrated; and further, 1 percent Communism can destroy this country. If 1 percent Communism can destroy us, and 100 percent Communism has not been able to make Russia work right, there must be something wrong with this country they haven't told us about. And if this country's top security could not keep the H-bomb out of Communist hands, how can we in the civil rights movement keep Communists from buying a $2.50 membership card?

For over ten years, college kids have been going to

Fort Lauderdale, Florida, during spring vacation. Each year, when they get there, they tear up the town. That is internal disorder. The police know when they are coming, what they will do, and make special provisions for handling the problem. That is an annual pattern. An annual pattern of internal disorder. But nobody blames the Communists for the trouble in Fort Lauderdale. They blame that trouble on growing pains; kids reaching maturity.

Then when the kids get back to school, they break into a girls' dormitory and take the panties out of the dresser drawers. They never take a pocketbook, lipstick or money. Is that a pattern or not? But nobody ever blames pantie raids on the Communists. Again people say it is growing pains; kids reaching maturity.

But when we go out and disrupt the peace, America says it is Communist-inspired. The truth is that civil rights demonstrations and riots are growing pains also. They are as natural as a woman giving birth to a baby. After nine months of growing pains, the baby will drop whether the woman is married or not, be she close to medical care or not, with or without Blue Cross or Blue Shield. Nature says there will be no baby without an act of sex. In like manner, without injustice and oppression, there will be no internal disorder. America's racial pregnancy is almost over, and that baby is going to fall even if it means death to the mother and the child. The Negro is America's baby. She gave birth to him in slavery, even as the first colonists were fleeing from oppression themselves. America should understand these growing pains of ours. They are not Communist-inspired. Rather, they are freedom-inspired. We have grown to a point where we want to eat freedom, sleep freedom, drink freedom, get drunk on freedom. And when you are drunk on freedom, you stumble across it when you least expect it.

Civil Rights Laws Are a Fraud

America did not give us any civil rights bill or voting rights bill out of the goodness of her heart. She resisted as long as she was allowed to resist. Finally she came through with a couple of bills and called it making progress. A couple of years ago, five white boys took it upon themselves to burn their draft cards. Immediately Congress passed an anti-draft card burning bill. But in a hundred years we have not been able to get an anti-lynching bill passed, making it a federal crime. So what my America told me in 1965 is that she cares more for a piece of cardboard than she does for my black momma. Because you can lynch my momma tonight but you better not burn a piece of cardboard. That is the progress you hear about.

Of course, civil rights bills are a fraud from the beginning. They are supposed to give me my rights and outlaw segregation. But when white America gets its rights under the United States Constitution and black America gets its rights under a civil rights bill, that is segregation. America has always been able to misuse me. Just when I start overcoming the system, a law appears which says it is illegal to segregate 60 percent of the housing in America. I have to resent that insult more than I did before.

Suppose someone cut off both of my ears. The government has no law to cover this injustice, no "anti-ear cutting law." So I go to the government, bleeding from both ears, and plead my case. "Would you please do something? This white boy just cut off both my ears." In response to my plea, a law is enacted which says it is only legal to cut off one ear. Now all of a sudden ear cutting becomes legal. Ear cutting did not come under the law at all before, now the cutting of one ear is legalized. I have to resent that.

Either you stop ear cutting completely, or don't bother to stop it partially.

It is the same with open housing, voting rights, or anything else. We demonstrated for voting rights long enough and loud enough for America to come up with a voting rights bill aimed at certain southern states. But there is more to voting rights than the right to vote. The northern Negro living in the ghetto has the right to vote, but he better pull the right switch. Just in case he doesn't remember which switch that is, the precinct captain will come around a few days before election and remind him. He will tell the man in the ghetto about what a shame it would be if the relief checks stopped coming in or if he were to be evicted from the housing projects. Intimidation which is used to force a man to vote "right" is just as bad as intimidation which keeps him from voting at all. Voting rights and the right to vote are not the same. If a man is not his own free agent when he pulls that switch, he does not have voting rights. He only has the worthless right to vote. But the voting rights bill does not cover the subtle intimidations of the North.

America did not wake up one morning with a change of heart and say together in unison, "We're so sorry for what we have been doing to the Negro." We got out into the streets and turned on the pressure and finally America began to respond. Now that the slow and long overdue response is beginning to come, everyone wants to give America credit. It is like a hungry man coming by my house while my family and I are having dinner. He tells me he is hungry, but I don't give him any food. For three days he sits at my table asking for food. But I still don't feed him. On the fourth day he pulls out a pistol and demands a meal. So I give it to him. The next week he comes by and goes through the same process all over again.

I refuse to feed him until I see that pistol. It is foolish for my neighbors to say that I am a good person for feeding that hungry man. If he hadn't pulled the pistol on me, he would have starved to death. I did not feed him out of the goodness of my heart; only in response to pressure. Do not be fooled into thinking that America would have given the Negro voting rights or anything else for any reason other than in response to pressure.

The only reason that we in the civil rights movement have been out here in the streets is to do the job which nobody else would do. If the church had been doing its job for the past hundred years, we would be saying "Thank God" today instead of "Thank the United States Supreme Court." I always hate to refer to those judges as the Supreme Court. I would prefer to call them our alternate sponsors.

Why Can't We Be Tax Collectors?

The federal government had all the power to grant civil rights. But instead the government looked at Negro leaders and said "go to it." The federal government willingly abdicated its responsibility to Negro leadership. When Negro leaders began making a few advances, forcing legislation which should have been initiated by the government in the first place, the government gave them credit for doing a tremendous job. If the government is going to require the civil rights movement to perform the basic governmental obligation of assuring equal rights for all citizens, then it ought to allow the movement to perform some other duties of government—like collecting taxes. The government is more than willing to collect the taxes but has to be pressured into granting civil rights. Human dignity is more important than all the money in the world because money cannot buy human dignity. Those who are called upon to perform the high calling of protectors of human dignity deserve to be entrusted with the lesser vocation of tax collectors.

The federal government demands the payment of man-made taxes but has to get somebody else to demand God-given rights. Not only Negro leadership, but also the Supreme Court has been used in this way. More than half of all legislation for human dignity has come about as a result of our demonstrations and Supreme Court decisions. The Supreme Court pushed the legislation through after we raised issues through demonstrations and civil disobedience. The President should have taken the initiative without relying on demonstrations and the Supreme Court. But the President has to run for reelection and he knows it. The Supreme Court has its job and doesn't have to worry about the voters. So if the Supreme Court pushes unpopular legislation through, nobody blames the President. He does not have to worry about reprisals at the polls. The Supreme Court does the President's unpopular work for him.

Now riots in the North are doing the same thing for local politicians that the Supreme Court does for the President. After a riot, a local politician can do some of the things he may have wanted to do all along. The riots give him an excuse and popular support. White folks don't complain and the local politician gets blame-free legislation.

Getting the civil rights movement to do part of the federal government's job makes about as much sense as Congress passing a law saying that all seventeen-year-old boys will be drafted; then bringing in a group of colored folks and saying, "All right, you go into those homes and bring in the new draftees." Those Negroes would be killed in the first house they entered. "Get my son," people would say. "You must be out of your mind. The government has a mechanism for getting their draftees. If the government wants my son, let it come and get him." The government also has a mechanism for assuring my rights —the United States Constitution. I want my rights under the same piece of paper that collects my taxes.

Those of us who have been struggling out in the streets of this nation are the true patriots. We have been fighting to uphold the Constitution. Everyone in America should be doing the same thing. I personally feel that anyone who does not uphold the Constitution is a traitor to his country. Our problem is not one of deciding how to kill Caesar. Rather it is a problem of making Caesar live up to his total responsibility. Any American who allows Caesar to collect his taxes has an obligation to see that Caesar does the rest of his job.

The day of partial payment in this country is drawing to a close. For a hundred years America has been changing the Negro's dollar for thirty-two cents. Now she wants to begin to make up for that injustice by offering sixty-four cents. We are out in the streets saying to our country, "A full dollar's change for a dollar spent. We are going to stop this country from cheating or the American cash register will ring no more."

Voting Power

In this struggle to force Caesar to fulfill all of his responsibilities, voting power is the most important weapon. The switch on the election machine is the only thing the modern Caesars really understand. And now Negroes all over the South have that switch in their hands. When they start pulling those switches, the current will be felt all over the world. The whole world is watching elections in America, especially in the South. Because the whole world knows it has not been treating black folks right. And what will be happening in elections in America will be previews of coming attractions for the rest of the world.

Not only will the whole world be watching American elections, it will be "overwatching." World opinion will take the liberty of deciding whether or not the Negro did a good job with his newly acquired voting rights. Careful calculation will try to determine how the new Negro vote affected the political fate of each candidate. But winning an election is not as important as being a part of one. The presence of the new Negro vote in the South will bring about changes quite apart from putting Negro-supported candidates into office. I am proud of the Negro voters in Alabama because they taught whites in that state how to peacefully protest. Whites knew they were faced with a formidable foe represented by the new Negro vote. So they went en masse to the polls and put George Wallace and his wife back into office. I would much rather see white supremacy upheld that way than with sticks and guns. For when bullets are replaced by ballots in a state where Negroes outnumber whites, white supremacy is on its way out.

When Negroes in the South become accustomed to their new voting power and start pulling those switches to their own advantage, there will be many little personal changes. When a Negro goes to work the morning after an election in which the black vote has proved itself a force to be reckoned with, the boss will say, "Come here, nigger." And tradition will compel the Negro to make the mistake of running to him. The white boss will blush and quickly say, "Oh, I'm not talking to you. I'm talking to my boy. My son, the nigger, that's who I want. As a matter of fact, we haven't been calling you nigger all these years.

We just didn't have the guts to say we were talking to someone else. We thought we were being nice by not embarrassing you with your mistake and letting you answer to the name nigger."

And I have a sneaking suspicion that there will be a lot of colored folks appearing all over the South who were supposed to be pure white. I can visualize a successful candidate and his wife sitting in their living room the evening after an election. The wife turns to her husband and says, "You know, dear, you wouldn't be in office tonight if those colored folks hadn't given you so many votes." And her husband will blush a little and say, "Well, honey, I've got something to say that I've been meaning to tell you for a long time. My grandma was colored."

It will not take the southern Negro as long to learn how to use his new voting rights as it did for him to acquire them. Negroes have been down under for so long that they have learned to pull themselves together overnight. They are used to getting their kids some new underwear or shoes and socks on Saturday night—just in time for church on Sunday morning. It doesn't take Negroes long to get themselves together once they know what they are going to do. And Negroes are going to vote.

When I speak at voting rallies in the South, I tell the new voters that now is the time to live up to the white folks' image of us. Throughout our lives we have heard white folks say, "All colored folks want to do is have fun; they're irresponsible." I think exercising the right to vote should be fun. We have been denied that right for so long we view the vote as something super secret and sacred. The same aura of mystery surrounds the polls as surrounds the church. But I tell those new voters in the South not to dress up to go to the polls as they would to go to church. Voting is a time to be yourself. Take off your wig and let the white voters see your real hair. Eat biscuits for breakfast and leave the syrup on your hands. Wear your work clothes and leave the mud on your overalls. Voting is your real right so do it as your real self! Be irresponsible and have fun. I hope individual Negroes are so busy before each election getting other people out to vote that they forget to vote themselves.

My only regret is that I am not a registered voter in Alabama or Mississippi. Each election I would be at the polls before early. I would be there fighting everyone who was ahead of me; just so that I could be the first person to shoot that juice through the machine. And I would bring a crowd with me; I'd bring a gang. "The more the merrier," people are fond of saying and there will be some happy times in future elections. The Negro vote is the only ballot that really counts; because it is the new one. And Caesar cannot predict what those happy Negroes will do!

VI

You have heard that it was said, "An eye for an eye and a tooth for a tooth." But I say to you, Do not resist one who is evil. But if any one strikes you on the right cheek, turn to him the other also.

MATTHEW 5:38–39

NONVIOLENT PROTEST
or
EYETOOTH REVOLUTION?

The Nuremberg trials brought the war criminals of Nazi Germany before the world court—from munitions makers, to generals, to prison guards. The justices of the world accused them of murder, of genocide. When the defendants pleaded that they were only obeying the laws of war and following orders, world justice declared that they were guilty and that man has a duty to disobey laws that are contrary to great moral laws.

Hegel, the German philosopher, said: "Truth is the absence of error, but it is known to be truth only because error has been experienced and truth has triumphed." Some form of civil disobedience is natural for men who seek truth after long periods of injustice. Man is born with a conscience. It matters little if you say this conscience is given by God or endowed by Nature. The conscience is still a basic part of man and cannot be wiped out.

The conscience of man realizes that laws are made for man and not for states to suppress or control man. Laws are to be used to create a climate of social behavior which is for the good and enrichment of the life of all men. When laws violate the nature of man, the natural order of life, they cannot be obeyed. Even if man is foolish enough to tolerate such laws, Nature herself will not respect them.

If white America passed a law saying that Negroes were not allowed to catch TB, cancer, or polio, there would be a law on the books officially, but Nature would not respect it. Negroes would be dying illegally all over the country! Until recently, there was a law on the books of nineteen states in America which said that Negroes could not marry white folks. Many people agreed with this law, but it violated the natural order. Such a law could not stand. What Nature fails to block, I defy man to try to resist. If Nature did not want me to have a white woman, she would have made her like a tree. I cannot have sex relations with a tree and a chicken cannot rape my momma. Since this marriage law was a violation of Nature, it eventually had to fall.

Sons of Liberty

And so it is also with laws which violate the nature of man; which violate a man's conscience. The Sons of Liberty who founded the United States of America realized that such laws must be disobeyed. And they were certainly not nonviolent in advocating civil disobedience. The Declaration of Independence deplores systems of oppression and sounds a stern word of warning to any governmental structure which would dare to violate man's nature.

"We hold these truths to be self-evident, that all men are created equal, that they are endowed by their Creator with certain unalienable Rights, that among these are Life, Liberty, and the pursuit of Happiness. That to secure these rights, Governments are instituted among Men, deriving their just powers from the consent of the governed. That whenever any Form of Government becomes destructive of these ends, it is the Right of the People to alter or to abolish it, and to institute new Government, laying its foundation on such principles and organizing its powers in such form, as to them shall seem most likely to effect their Safety and Happiness." So reads America's birth certificate, the Declaration of Independence.

So seriously did the American patriots take these words that they not only refused to pay taxes to the Mother Country but they took her tea and dumped it into the water. Such an act was a violent refusal to tolerate a system of oppression and injustice; a legal system which violated the nature of man. That moment in history is remembered in *every* school in America, both in the black ghetto and the white suburb, as the Boston Tea Party.

In the streets of the black ghettos all over America today, there is a violent reaction to a system of oppression which violates the nature of man. America's black ghettos are shameful symbols of poverty and squalor in the midst of prosperity. Benjamin Franklin recognized the injustice of poverty and knew what it would do to a man. He wrote: "Poverty often deprives a man of all virtue. It is hard for an empty bag to stand upright." He was also the author of the slogan for the American Revolution, whose symbol was a snake cut into pieces, "Join or Die!"

As with the Declaration of Independence, the slogan of the American Revolution was a violent reminder that laws violating the nature of man must be changed. If the violence of the Sons of Liberty is commemorated in American history as the Boston Tea Party, the revolt in Watts or Detroit should be known in future history books as the Saturday Night Fish Fry.

The passage of time and technological advance also demand a change in the law. When the Duryea brothers put the first two automobiles on the market in the state of Ohio, laws were needed to govern the operation of two automobiles. The worst the law had to consider was a wreck between two automobiles. The passage of time and the development of production techniques has brought about mass murder on the highways of America. The new situation demands a change in the law.

The passage of time and an increase in travel demands a uniformity in traffic laws throughout the country. Suppose I have been driving all of my life in the state of California. It is legal for me to make a right-hand turn on a red light. Then I rent a car and drive to Chicago. The first time I make a right-hand turn on a red light in Chicago the cop is standing ready to hand me a summons. There is no sign telling me I *cannot* make the right-hand turn I have been used to making all my life. Nor did Hertz rent me a car whose brakes would jam when I tried to make the right-hand turn in Chicago. Justice demands uniformity of traffic laws.

Since laws which violate the conscience of man *must* be changed, the crucial question is how the change will be effected. When the presentation of just grievances, either at the conference table or through nonviolent demonstration, are unheeded, some form of civil disobedience is inevitable. Even in a nonviolent revolution it is necessary to use guerrilla warfare tactics; that is, open violation of the existing laws of society. Such civil disobedience should be open and nonsecret. It should be an expression of man's conscience willfully disobeying laws which violate the nature of man. Persons who engage in acts of civil disobedience should be willing to suffer the penalty imposed by the unjust law, both to demonstrate the injustice of the law and to show a respect for law and order when it operates within a framework of justice. Those who engage in acts of civil disobedience are not saying they do not want laws. They are saying that they want laws to be based on justice for all men.

How to Avoid Riots

During the summer of 1965, I was Peck's Bad Boy in Chicago, according to the press. For a solid month I led nonviolent marches in the city of Chicago. For thirty-one days straight, I boarded a plane each morning in San Francisco, where I was playing a nightclub engagement at the Hungry i, and flew to Chicago to lead afternoon marches. Then I flew back to San Francisco each evening to go to work. Why did I commute four thousand miles each day for thirty-one days? Because I knew that if the city was being hit by nonviolent demonstrations, there was less chance of rioting in the streets. The nonviolent demonstration gives the ghetto dweller a ray of hope that perhaps the power structure will hear his just demands and do something to alleviate the problems.

It was a real struggle to keep the demonstration alive. If I had not known that this was the only way to avoid violence, I might have been discouraged. I saw my four- and six-year-old daughters get arrested that summer. Think about that. When demonstrators are arrested, the men are taken one place, the women another, and the children still another. My children had never been away from their home and their mother overnight.

But if I ever had any question about being able to justify involving my kids in demonstrations they were answered by my little four-year-old daughter Lynne. When we were being placed in the wagon to go to jail, Lynne said to me, "We're in trouble, aren't we, Daddy?" That night, I cried because of what she said. Tears of anger, really. I was angry that my momma and daddy had not taught me I was in trouble at the age of four. I didn't find out until I was twenty-nine. And here my little four-year-old daughter had a twenty-five-year head start on her father.

We all know of times when kids have been used for wrong. In election frauds in the City of Chicago, kids have voted. And if I read my Bible right, little David was only a boy when he went out to fight Goliath with a slingshot. I was not asking my kids to kill anybody, only to stand up for what was right. And there is no age limit on that.

My wife had a baby that summer on June 16. Since we were running out of demonstrators, I called her on June 18 and said, "Come on out of the hospital, baby, because we are running out of demonstrators and we can't stop this thing now." As long as we held nonviolent demonstrations, there were no riots in the city of Chicago. Even when we were arrested en masse, in acts of civil disobedience halting downtown traffic, there was no violence. Only when the demonstrations stopped did violence erupt on the West Side of Chicago.

Violence results when the power structure fails to respond to the peaceful, nonviolent demonstration. Not only does the power structure fail to consider the just demands of nonviolent demonstrators, it will try to defame and ridicule nonviolent leaders. I was arrested that summer and accused of biting a cop. I stood trial and lost my case. The story of how I lost my case is a study in governmental mockery.

The woman who actually bit the cop came to me and offered to testify on my behalf. I knew she bit the cop; the cop knew she bit him. The trouble came when city hall found out she bit him. The woman was given a job with the poverty program, paying $175 per week, with the stipulation that she not testify in court. The biter is now making more money than the bitten!

There is a pattern of governmental refusal to listen to just demands. The summer riot season in Chicago in 1966 began in the Puerto Rican neighborhood. Many people in Chicago have always wondered why there were no Puerto Rican cops. The official answer from city hall has been, "We don't have anything against Puerto Ricans, but the official height standard for Chicago policemen is five feet, ten inches. Puerto Ricans are just too short."

If Puerto Rican leaders go to city hall and ask that the height requirements be lowered three inches to allow more Puerto Ricans to become policemen, they will be politely but firmly refused. After the Puerto Ricans threw bricks in their neighborhood for three days, the height requirement *was* lowered three inches—an inch per day of rioting. If the riots had lasted a month, there would be job openings on the Chicago police force for Spanish-speaking midgets!

It is a shame that it should take rioting to get Puerto Rican policemen in Chicago. The need for Spanish-speaking policemen in Puerto Rican neighborhoods is crucial. Imagine the problem of communication which is created when the cop on the beat does not understand your language. A man whose wife has just been scalded and seriously burned comes running out of his apartment, grabs the cop, and yells excitedly at him in Spanish. The cop reacts by grabbing his nightstick because he doesn't understand what the excitement is all about.

After the rioting in the Puerto Rican neighborhoods settled down during the summer of 1966, the West Side of Chicago blew up. It is ironic that the rioting in the colored neighborhood started over some water. Negro leaders had been politely asking city hall for some swimming pools. And city hall turned a deaf ear to them. So the residents of the ghetto decided to create their own swimming pools by turning on the fire hydrants. When the cops came to shut the hydrants off, the trouble started. It seems strange to me that white folks should want to cut off the water in a colored neighborhood. They have been trying to run away from hot nigger stink for a hundred years. Instead of turning off the water, they should have brought in some soap.

Since the bricks were thrown all over the West Side of Chicago, it is hard now to walk in that section without stepping into a swimming pool. The government conveniently found forty million dollars after the rioting which did not seem to be available before. It was the same pattern in Los Angeles. Before the rioting, few people had ever heard of the Watts section of Los Angeles. After the bricks were thrown, some two hundred million dollars were poured into that community in emergency funds. As nonviolent demonstrations help to avoid violence in the streets, the refusal of government to respond to the just demands of such demonstrations creates an atmosphere of anger, frustration, and desperation which assures a violent reaction.

Pay Attention, America!

Acts of civil disobedience, whether they are nonviolent demonstrations or riots, are attempts to get America's attention. If I am talking and you want to get my attention, you will say in a normal tone of voice, "Dick Gregory." If I pay no attention to you, you will say in a much louder voice, "Dick Gregory." If I still refuse to listen to you, you will stand in front of me so that I cannot avoid seeing you. If everything else fails to get my attention, you will finally grab me and shake me and say,

"Dick Gregory, listen to me." The chances are I will listen to what you have to say. The throwing of bricks in the ghettos of the nation is the shaking of the foundations of America so that she must listen to the grief of her black children.

I have learned many valuable lessons from my own black children. I have learned, for example, that I cannot expect unreasonable discipline. I must consider the legitimate demands of my children. If I stay out most of the night and come home drunk, feeling good or bad, it is unreasonable for me to expect my children to be quiet around the house until I am ready to get up. Once when I was sleeping soundly my children came into the bedroom at eight o'clock in the morning and started to play. Naturally I shouted my disapproval. My little seven-year-old daughter said to me, "Daddy, I know you have to sleep. But we also have to grow up. If you are going to come into this house while we are growing up, I would suggest you take us out with you at night. If we come in as late as you do, the chances are we will not want to get up before you. But Momma puts us to bed at seven o'clock, so you have to expect us to make noise early in the morning."

When one of my babies cries, I know she is crying for a reason. Even though I may be annoyed by the crying, it does not make sense for me to shout at the baby to stop crying. Perhaps my wife and I have been out late and have neglected to change the diaper or changed it too hurriedly so that the diaper pin is sticking the baby in the rump. The baby doesn't get any more out of crying than I do. She doesn't want to cry, but crying is her only way of getting my attention and telling me that something is wrong. The louder I scream at the baby, the louder she cries. She will cry until I remove the diaper pin or gangrene sets in and the baby dies. The only way I can stop the crying is to remove the cause of the crying.

Rioting is the cry of the ghetto. It is an attention-getting device reminding America that infection has set in and death approaches. It makes no more sense for America to say, "Stop rioting" to the ghetto than it does for the parent to say, "Stop crying" to the baby. Remove the cause that is inflicting the wound and the crying will cease and not before. Nature has a way of warning the body that death approaches. The wise man will heed the warning. If you have a splitting headache, you recognize the danger signal and go to the doctor. Perhaps the doctor investigates and finds you have brain cancer. If the doctor tells you instead that you have a migraine headache and prescribes some aspirin, you are relieved. The doctor has told you what you *want* to hear. But you will still die. There is a difference between what you *want* to hear and what you *must* hear.

Each nonviolent demonstration has been a warning signal of America's cancer. It is a symptom that needs diagnosis. But the diagnosis must be honest. Even cancer can be cured if checked and caught in time. If America is told that she only has a migraine headache and not a malignant tumor, she will be temporarily relieved but the country will perish. The body of America must submit to a thorough examination so that the germ which multiplies within can be destroyed. Unless government faces an honest diagnosis and invests all of its resources on a thorough cure, the infection will spread all over America and death is sure.

The Recovery of Manhood

America has heard what she wanted to hear and is now being forced to listen to what she must hear. When

America heard Martin Luther King preaching nonviolence she was temporarily relieved because "turn the other cheek" sounded better to her than "an eye for an eye and a tooth for a tooth." But the failure to respond to "turn the other cheek" demonstrations has produced the "eye for an eye" revolution.

Nonviolence was necessary to set the revolution in motion. For hundreds of years the Negro has lived under a system of oppression which stripped him of his manhood. The only thing left to the Negro was his cowardice. He could only pick up a gun and kill when white folks told him to do it. I am grateful to Martin Luther King because he gave me back my manhood. When Dr. King began preaching nonviolent resistance, he appealed to my cowardice. In the process of going and confronting wrong nonviolently, I got my manhood back. The mistreatment I suffered while standing for the right nonviolently tested my manhood.

Suppose I get on a bus in Chicago with my seven-year-old daughter. We sit down in the seat across from you. What you do not know is that my daughter has just stabbed and killed my wife. I am taking her to the police station because I do not want the cops coming to my apartment. Suppose all of a sudden my daughter whispers in my ear, "Daddy, if Momma isn't dead, I'm going to stab her again." Enraged, I take my fist and hit my little seven-year-old daughter. You have not heard what she said, nor do you know what has happened back at my apartment. All you see is the grown brutal man hitting a little seven-year-old girl. When you see me do that, you will grab me, because I have tested your manhood.

Negroes have been lynched for hundreds of years, but no one ever picked up a brick or a Molotov cocktail because of it. But when the northern ghetto brother saw white America mishandling nonviolent demonstrators, his manhood was tested. And his reaction of outrage is the same as yours would be seeing me hit my little girl on the bus.

America mistreated nonviolence by giving it a racist interpretation. America interpreted nonviolence to mean that Negroes were not going to hit white folks. When Negroes said they were nonviolent in civil rights demonstrations, America applauded. But when Martin Luther King, Stokely Carmichael or Muhammad Ali pushes the nonviolent philosophy to its extreme, saying Negroes should not fight in America's war, the country was outraged. America approved nonviolence for Negro demonstrators and equally approved the violence which killed Malcolm X. America is forever demonstrating her respect for violence. The white power structure forced black people to love Malcolm X. Martin Luther King said, "Love your fellow man and turn the other cheek," and he was called a nigger and a Communist and thrown in jail. Malcolm X said, "Get a gun and defend yourself, the pink-eyed devils need to be dead." He was not arrested nor was he thrown in jail, because America respects the man with a gun.

Nonviolence: The Two-Edged Sword

Nonviolence is a two-edged sword which can be a preface to violence. Gandhi's nonviolent movement in India was a gathering of people before the violence of independence. In the same way in the civil rights movement, the threat of a violent alternative produced support for nonviolent involvement. Many Negroes excused themselves from participation in the struggle by saying, "I would like to go to Alabama but I am not nonviolent. If someone hits me, I'm going to hit them back." When Malcolm X appeared on the scene, the old excuse did not work any more. Violence could not be an excuse for nonparticipation. Negroes who felt they had to hit back could be told to go join Malcolm X. In most cases those same Negroes would decide to stay with Martin Luther King for a while.

For over a hundred years, the Negro in America ran from the white man. And nine times out of ten he got away. But the Negro was so busy running scared, he ran past an education, decent employment, and adequate housing. When a brother was lynched in the South, Negroes resented him for slowing up. It is a strange truth that a Negro is not lynched by a white man but rather by his own attitude. If two Negroes are confronted by a group of whites and they stand and fight it out, their death is called murder. But if the Negroes turn and run, when the white mob catches them and kills them, it is called lynching. Only the man who runs can be lynched.

When the Negro ran from the white man and made it to the safety of hiding in the bushes, he was so glad to be safe that he forgot to hate his chaser. A few years ago, the nonviolent philosophy told the Negro to stop running; confront the man who is chasing you, and turn the other cheek. When the Negro stops running, his fear is gone. He has turned the other cheek and been hit twice. Now that Negro is mad. And there is a big difference between a scared Negro and a mad Negro.

The nonviolent philosophy stopped the Negro in his tracks. He will no longer run from a system of oppression which violates the nature of man. The conscience of black America will demand a change in the system through whatever means are necessary. Such is the spirit of revolution.

For too long America has attempted to avoid the inevitable change by changing the name instead. The spirit of unrest in America was called "a Negro Problem," a "Movement" or a "Demonstration." What is happening in America today is none of these things. It is a revolution. And it is not a Negro Revolution. It is an American Revolution; the Second American Revolution. The spirit of revolutionary change is sweeping this country whose principles and ideals were firmly articulated in the Declaration of Independence.

Queen Liliuokalani of Hawaii wrote to the United States Government at the time of her country's acquisition in protest:

"It is a rule of common law that the acts of any person deprived of civil rights have no force nor weight, either at law or in equity. . . ."

We eventually made Hawaii a full state in our republic. The Negro too demands his state: the state of full citizenship and human dignity. We delude ourselves if we believe this is a struggle for civil rights. It is a revolution for human rights. In Panama, the Panamanian set fire to the American Embassy, burned the American flag, and told the American to get out. America did not declare him to be a criminal. Nor did she demand stricter law enforcement. Instead of demanding tougher legislation to maintain law and order, America sent top diplomats to Panama to listen to their leaders. Eventually America split the canal with Panama. We did not call what happened in Panama "mob action" but rather "legitimate protest." The Negro in America wants the white man to split the country with him. He just wants his fair share of the American Dream.

Laws which violate the nature of man, and a system supported and perpetrated by those laws, must and will be changed.

Some day there will be a Great Trial, be it in Heaven or in China. I do not know if we will be judged by the angels or the Chinese. But at that Great Trial, I want to be able to plead "not guilty" to obeying laws against humanity.

VII

For they have sown the wind,
And they shall reap the whirlwind.

HOSEA 8:7

For I have seen violence and strife in the town,
Day and night they encircle upon her walls,
And trouble and toil are within her;
Ruin is within her;
Oppression and fraud do not depart from her market-place.

PSALMS 55:9–11

WINDY CITIES

I have seen violence and strife in cities from one end of the country to the other. I have seen American cities left in ruins because oppression and fraud do not depart from their market places. And on Friday, August 13, 1965, just before dawn, I was shot during the revolution which swept through the Watts section of Los Angeles. Some people called it a riot. The insurance companies called it an "insurrection" at first to take advantage of escape clauses in their policies. Many Negroes called it a resurrection. But it was a natural revolution, Nature's response to the violation of the nature of man.

I have been out of America seven times and I am thirty-four years old. Every time I leave America I am embarrassed; because only seven times in my life have I been asked to write the word American beside my name. When I leave my country and I fill out a customs card in a foreign country, I am not asked to identify myself by color or race but rather by nationality. If I held up a bank anywhere in America, the newspapers would say that a Negro robbed a bank. But if I held up a bank in France, it would be reported as an American who committed the crime. I have to leave my country to be an American hoodlum.

It seems strange that the closer we are to a problem the less we are able to see it. People in Los Angeles called the revolution in Watts the Watts riot. People in San Francisco called it the Los Angeles riot. People in New York and Chicago called it the California riot. In Europe it was known as the American riot. And if there had been anyone on the moon, they would have probably called it the Earth Rumble.

I cannot help but feel that you have to be outside of America to realize where the problem lies. If the great social problem which is sweeping this nation existed in any other country in the world, America could solve it. We have the financial resource and the knowledge. All that is lacking is the will.

People speak of the tragedy of thirty churches being blown up in Mississippi. But if a Jewish temple is destroyed in Moscow, we would refer to the outrage in Russia. And people say how terrible it was that James Meredith was shot in Mississippi. James Meredith was shot in America. If I go to Russia tomorrow, I do not have to worry about being shot on the street corner, because I know that Russia would not dare allow it to happen. Russia knows that America would not stand for it. The only reason I can get shot and killed, or hit with a brick or a bottle anywhere in this country, is because America *will* stand for it.

But Nature will *not* stand for it. Nature follows a pattern of evolution. Evolution is the process of gradual, internal, natural change. Turning things around by the application of external force produces revolution, which is Nature's response to the attempt to thwart the evolutionary process. When I speak of external forces causing revolution, I do not mean "outside agitators" as many people do, including Billy Graham and former Los Angeles Police Chief Parker. A true revolution is a struggle against conflicts from within, and the external forces are the forces of

Nature. I do not mean the weather, which many people believe is a factor in the eruption of already combustible material, but the nature of man. People try to place the blame for rioting on anonymous "outside agitators" in order to avoid facing their own responsibilities. But there are not enough Communists in all of Russia to stand on every street corner in America and wait for an incident where a Negro is arrested by a cop in a manner which will tip off a riot.

The Hand of Oppression

The external force which causes revolution is the hand of oppression. The outbreak of violence in Watts, Newark or Detroit is the inevitable expression of a nonviolent revolution faced with force and suppression. Each revolution is caused by problems specific to the particular area, but those problems are common to all American cities in the crowded, hopeless, miserable Negro ghettos. Sociologists, psychologists, and ex-directors of the CIA can analyze these causes. It is a pattern, as familiar as the imprint of a hand: Unemployment, high-density population, substandard living conditions, deep wounds of discrimination, and police brutality. These are the four fingers and thumb which anyone can recognize as a human hand. But each person individually has his own personal reason to strike out against society, the society which has reduced him to his state of antisocial agony; just as, upon microscopic examination, each individual's fingerprints are seen to be unique.

If it were possible to do a case study of each individual who participated in riots anywhere in this country, you would find that each individual was in the street for a different reason. Each person has suffered different denials. The same employer who refused me a job did not necessarily turn down the Negro who is throwing the brick. But he was turned down by another employer. I have a personal gripe or embarrassment because I have suffered the indignity of being called "nigger" or "boy" by a particular white man. Another Negro did not suffer exactly the same indignity as I did but has been called "nigger" and "boy" by a different white man, using a different tone of voice. Thus his frustrations are different than mine. Each individual Negro is imprinted by his own personal experience of indignity and the combined resentment causes revolution.

The problem can only be solved when the hand of oppression is recognized. Rioting in the ghetto is best seen as the imprint of a hand reaching out to grab something which rightfully belongs to the man with the brick, but which has been denied him. When America truly recognizes this hand, it is possible for her to reach out and take the rioter by the hand instead of trying to track down each riot participant like a criminal by his fingerprints.

The Thunder of Judgment

When the hand of oppression is applied to the nature of man, disturbing the evolutionary process, it is Nature who must be answered. Nature applies the judgment. America has sown the wind of oppression and she shall reap the whirlwind of judgment. When the rioting in Watts first erupted, some people were prompted to call it a natural disaster. Few understood how accurately they described it. The man in the ghetto may be underfed, uneducated, unemployed, hot in the summer and cold in the winter, but he is as *weak* as a hurricane. The black ghettos of America represent the power of Nature. When hot air meets cold air there is an explosion. We call it thunder.

Thunder has been rumbling over this land for a long time and many have pretended to themselves that because it did not rain there would be no storm. America has preferred to ignore the thunder. She made no preparations, took no precautions, just pretended that the thunder would cease and the storm would blow away.

Now the storm is upon us. It is a hurricane and the winds of destruction are leveling cities from one end of the country to the other. The violence of Watts was pointedly demonstrated by Nature as minor compared to the force of hurricane Betsy which swept California a few weeks later. The hurricane has been whirling all around America since a Negro seamstress named Rosa Lee Parks was just too tired to walk to the back of the bus in Montgomery, Alabama. There is calm in the eye of the hurricane. The eye of this social whirlwind has been the nonviolent concentration of the storm in peaceful protests across the land. But America has refused to recognize nonviolence as part of the storm. She has tried to push herself out of the eye, which is also the eye of the world. Now the first winds are beginning to blow.

Twenty or thirty years ago, the Negro spoke out. Today Nature is speaking out. America found it very convenient not to listen to the Negro and she thought she was getting away with her folly. But America was merely sowing the wind and now she is forced to listen to the whirlwind.

We do not blame the weatherman for hurricanes. It is his job to tell us about the approaching disaster and help us prepare for it. Why then does America insist on blaming Negro leadership for the violence in the ghetto? Negro leaders have been trying to be good weathermen. They have been telling America of the approaching storm; they have prescribed precautionary measures, but they have been ignored, vilified, abused, jailed, and beaten. Should Negro leadership be blamed for issuing the storm warning? At the time of the eruption of violence in Watts, former Police Chief Parker laid the blame on Negro leadership. In January, 1962, Chief Parker spoke at a meeting sponsored by the John Birch Society called "Project Alert." Would it be the fault of the John Birch Society if the Communist takeover it predicts might some day come to pass?

Negro leaders have the eloquence to explain to the people and to the government the nature of the Negro's needs. The man in the ghetto listens to his leader ask, and ask, and ask again. When he sees this leader rejected, defamed, humiliated, and cheated, then it is often the leader who is blamed rather than the system which abuses him. By her refusal to listen and act, America has caused moderate Negro leadership to be rejected by the black ghettos.

The Negro leaders say, "Give us better schools, integrated education, better housing, decent, meaningful employment, the literal translation of the Constitution." The man in the ghetto will not be able to list his needs any more than a sick man can diagnose his own ills. He just knows that it hurts. Ask the man in the ghetto what he wants and he will tell you: "Nuttin!" And when he says nothing he means everything. To express the inexpressible he makes his mark like an illiterate man makes an X instead of writing his name. The man in the ghetto makes his mark with a brick. He knows that America cannot ignore his inarticulate brick the way she ignored the eloquence of his leaders. Such is the way of Nature. Man may ignore the prognostications of charts and diagrams, but the fury of the storm itself is inescapable. They have sown the wind, and they shall reap the whirlwind.

Give Us a Drink of Water

The Negro did not create the storm, any more than a man dying of thirst in the desert made the land arid. Nature created the desert. The Negro is dying from the lack of constitutional justice owed him by Nature in an American desert, while all around him other Americans thrive in the oasis. The Negro not only loves America, he is parched for her. His is not a revolution for property, but for rights. This thirsty determination can be seen as a revolution for a glass of water.

The white man in America has held the full glass of water and denied the Negro a drink from the same glass. The Negro does not want to take the glass away from the white man; he is merely demanding his rightful share of the contents. He knows that if he is forced to fight, the glass will be knocked from the white man's hand and, not only will freedom be spilled for both, but the glass itself will be broken. If the white man does not give up half, he will lose it all. This is why Negro leadership has been asking, politely and humbly, "Please give us our half of freedom."

But America has not only refused the Negro a drink of the American Dream, she has had the nerve to rattle the ice cubes in his face. Little black kids in the ghetto school are teased with the words of Jefferson, Franklin, and Tom Paine. America has let the Negro look at the Constitution, but has refused to let him taste it. Now America is willing to give the Negro a little, to feed him with an eye dropper, a little at a time until the constitution of the Negro is "ready for it."

But the whirlwinds of Nature will not permit such an insult. Nature will prevail. Even though the Negro knows that a violent struggle may spill the whole, Nature will make him fight for it. If the glass of America's liberty is shattered in such a revolution, who is to blame? When we have all perished in this parched land, will we blame the man who fought for his share, the man who refused to share, or Nature, who made both the man and the water and decreed that one must have the other to live or else die?

Too Free to Be Patient

There are those who refuse to accept the laws of Nature and ask, "Why does the Negro act the way he is acting, when he is better off today than ever before?" I can somewhat understand white America asking this question, because as a kid I could never understand why white folks committed suicide. Then I grew up and became a successful Negro in America (rather than an American who became successful). Only then could I understand why rich white folks commit suicide. And it is the same reason the Negro is acting the way he is today and why the title of Martin Luther King's book is such an important reminder to America, *Why We Can't Wait.*

The ultimate aim of life is death. There are two elements which let you know if you are alive or dead—joy and pain. The more joy you are able to experience, the more vulnerable you are to pain. The more opportunity to indulge joy you are entitled to, the more you are exposed to the pain of its loss or the agony of its unfulfillment. Only the mother who has the joy of a baby can experience the pain of the loss of a child. Only the man who has experienced the joy of love can know the pain of its loss. Only the man who can enjoy the pleasure and convenience of a plane ride risks the pain of an airline crash.

When I was a kid on relief in the ghetto of St. Louis

and I got hungry, I only wanted beans and cornbread because that was all I knew. Today if I get hungry, my appetite is harder to satisfy. I have tasted a variety of foods, experienced the joy of fine restaurants and special cooking. A poor man wants no more than a pair of shoes. A rich man has traveled all over the world and knows the pain of boredom. He is constantly searching for a new place to go. Since I know what it is to travel first class on an airplane, I am uncomfortable if the plane is full and I have to ride tourist.

As the Negro is exposed to more freedom, more rights, he knows the pain of deprivation from *all* that he is entitled to. If he is willing to die for full liberty, he is no more of a madman than Patrick Henry. America is the rich man on the verge of committing suicide.

Violence Is the Voice of the Black Ghetto

The violent natural whirlwind is the voice of the black ghetto. The voice of violence is heard in cities all over America today, not only because nonviolent voices have been ignored, mocked or forcefully silenced, but also because violence is the voice that America has taught the ghetto. America is a violent teacher. We commit murder in the name of government by permitting capital punishment. That is violent. We induct young men into the armed services, instruct them in the use of weapons, teach them to kill, and tell them that it is honorable to wage war. That is violent instruction. We place violent people in positions of "peace officers," with cattle prods and tear gas as their tools for keeping the peace. For a hundred years we have permitted lynchings. When the Negro cried out for an anti-lynching bill, saying, "Please, please stop the violence," America explained that such a law would be unconstitutional. We permitted civil rights workers to be intimidated, kidnaped, and killed. We permitted churches to be bombed and children disintegrated. We have burned babies in Alabama and in Vietnam. Is it any wonder that the violent whirlwind haunts America with the echo, "Burn, baby, burn"? America has sown the wind of violence and she shall reap the whirlwind of destruction.

Even the looting and theft which are a part of the social whirlwind destroying American cities remind us of a hurricane. There is always looting after natural disasters, tornadoes, floods, earthquakes, and hurricanes, and it is necessary to call in the National Guard to keep the theft in check. People deprived of justice, which is the norm for law and order among men, will take what Nature delivers in this absence like the children of Israel took manna from heaven. Only a law of justice supersedes animal instincts. A higher moral law can overrule natural instinct. A Muslim will not steal pork. A true Christian will not blow up a church.

Killing also is a part of every natural disaster. Nature kills without regard to person or circumstance. A tornado will blow a roof off a house and it will miss the wino in the gutter and hit the pregnant woman and kill her. Yet America is shocked by the reports of killing in the riot-torn areas. Killing itself does not bother America. There is more killing on the highway over a holiday weekend than in all the riots to date. Negro deaths are not ordinarily even reported in white newspapers. Violence of one Negro against another is not even considered newsworthy. Violence of white men against Negroes is not very shocking to America either. What alarms the white man is not simply violence, but the thought that the violence he has taught the Negro may be turned upon himself.

The Negro lives with violence every day; violence to his human dignity. He learns the violence of being told he cannot go to a good school, and then being told he cannot get a good job because he hasn't been to a good school, and then again being told that he can't go to a good hotel or restaurant because he hasn't the money, or the clothes, or the manners the other two would have given him. America has never calculated the mental and emotional violence it has sown in her Negro minority through discrimination. America is only able to calculate in physical life and dollars. The whirlwinds of social revolution are helping to estimate the damages.

When the Negro has individually surmounted all the wounds of discrimination and got himself an education, earned himself a job, and made enough money to be able to afford the fruits of American society, then he meets physical violence, the same violence he thought he would escape through his sweat and tears. He is told that he cannot buy a house in a better neighborhood, even with all his money. It is a violent reminder to the Negro in the ghetto that he may not still be a slave, but he is yet a serf, indentured to the land.

The white man does not know the wind of violence he has sown in the black community and he does not want to know. His newspapers do not carry the news which would inform him, but the Negro knows even if his newspapers do not carry the news either. Not one white man in Los Angeles knows that the temper for the riot in Watts was set by the rape of a Negro woman by a white cop. Yet it is so. He pulled her out of the car in which she was riding with a friend and threatened them both. Then he took her into the police car and raped her. And now that you have heard this, as the entire community of Watts heard it, do not deceive yourself by saying that perhaps I am making it up. It can be verified.

And if you accept the validity of the story, do not

further delude yourself by rationalizing that it is an "isolated incident" and "one bad apple does not make a rotten carload." If it had happened to a white woman you would have heard it and been outraged. And it is not an isolated incident. Earlier in the year *another* Los Angeles cop raped *another* Negro girl under almost identical circumstances, and *that* incident was well known in Watts and unknown in Beverly Hills. Negroes are not shocked because they have known for years that black women were subject to the physical outrage of any white man with authority, from the plantation owner of yesterday to the cop of today.

During the summer of 1966, in Fort Pierce, Florida, a five-year-old Negro girl was raped by a white employee of a Headstart program financed by anti-poverty funds. Letters were written to President Johnson, Sargent Shriver, and Governor Hayden Burns. The incident was hushed up rather than investigated. A Negro girl subjected to physical outrage by one white man in authority was ignored by white men in the highest positions of authority.

Run, Whitey, Run

When the indignities which the Negro has suffered at the hands of the cop are recognized, is it not amazing that more cops are not killed in riots? Magazine articles following the rioting in Newark and Detroit raised this question. They questioned whether snipers were really shooting to kill. The answer is that they were not. When the sniper shot he did not shoot at the National Guard because he has no war with the Army. The green uniform is the same one he wore himself, along with his father, brother, and cousin. The American Army has helped more Negroes than it has harmed. It has taught Negroes that they could eat, sleep, study, and fight as good as any white man and right along with him. The Army has sent the Negro to school and taught him he deserves some dignity. As much as the Negro hates the blue uniform of the cop, the sniper did not shoot to kill him. The Negro does not want to see the white man die. He sees white folks die every night on the television screen. What the Negro has never seen is a white man run. The snipers were shooting to make the white man run and hide. And he ran!

It is my hope that the white man in America keeps running, back to his history books, his philosophy books, and his Bible, all the way back to those documents he keeps in his libraries but does not read and no longer believes. I hope the white man in America doesn't stop running until he gets to the Declaration of Independence and the United States Constitution, those documents for which the first American Revolution was fought. Perhaps then he will let the Negro share the rewards of that first victory and spare our beloved land the violence of a second revolution.

More than a hundred years ago, in Edwardsville, Illinois, in 1858, Abraham Lincoln was speaking to a group of white folks. If he spoke those same words today on the Peter Jennings or Walter Cronkite news report on television, he would be arrested for inciting to riot. His words make Stokely Carmichael sound like a moderate. Lincoln said: "When you have succeeded in dehumanizing the Negro; when you have put him down and made it impossible for him to be but as the beasts of the field; when you have extinguished his soul in this world and placed him where the ray of hope is blown out as in the darkness of the damned, are you quite sure the demon you have aroused will not turn and rend you?"

Lincoln knew well the foundation of liberty which must

undergird America. And he foresaw the decay of the foundations of this nation. He concluded: "Our reliance is in the love of liberty which God has planted in us. Our defense is in the preservation of the spirit which prizes liberty as the heritage of all men, in all lands everywhere. Destroy this spirit and you have planted the seeds of despotism at your own doors. Familiarize yourself with the chains of bondage, and you are preparing your own limbs to wear them. Accustomed to trample on the rights of others, you have lost the genius of your own independence, and become the fit subjects of the first cunning tyrant who rises among you."

VIII

Do not be anxious about your life, what you shall eat or what you shall drink, nor about your body, what you shall put on. Is not life more than food, and the body more than clothing? . . . Your heavenly Father knows that you need them all. But seek first his kingdom and his righteousness, and all these things shall be yours as well.

MATTHEW 6:25, 32–33

THE SHOE'S TOO TIGHT

The basic problem of men and nations is man's inhumanity to his fellow man. A frightening thought occurred to me one day as to how America could end the war in Vietnam immediately. It is frightening because it illustrates the inhumane disregard man has for his brother.

The solution to the war in Vietnam would require bringing all of the American troops back home. But the withdrawal should be done secretly. And instead of complete and total withdrawal, the troops should be replaced with animals—cocker spaniels, parakeets, chimpanzees, and Siamese cats. When the animal lovers in America woke up one morning and read that we had animals in Vietnam instead of American boys, they would storm the White House in protest. America will tolerate the taking of human life without giving it a second thought. But don't misuse a household pet.

Man's inhumanity to his fellow man is not a matter of race. Go to Skid Row and take a good look at those drunks lying in the gutter, day in and day out. I am talking about that man who has been lying on the sidewalk so long that he looks like he is growing out of it. You cannot tell where the sidewalk ends and he begins. Such a sight turns my stomach. Because I know that if a horse stumbled and fell in the same spot where the poor drunk is lying, society would not permit that horse to lie on the sidewalk. The horse would be removed within a half-hour. If a dog is hit by a car on a city street, the Humane Society is on the scene immediately. They do not check the dog's pocket to see if he has proper identification or Blue Cross and Blue Shield. The dog is picked up and taken away. Only human beings are left lying on the sidewalk days on end.

Even man's attempts at moral action are frequently inhumane. When confronted with the problem of starvation in India, the United States appropriated $688 million in aid to India to fight famine. When you count the population of India, you will realize that the appropriation is a dollar per Indian. Is it any wonder that India had to turn to Russia for aid?

Though man misuses his brother and continually suppresses the underdog, Nature has a beautiful way of intervening on behalf of the oppressed. Jesus reminded us of this fact of life when he taught that it is futile to worry about food, shelter, clothing, and preserving one's life. All of these things are under the control of a power higher than man. It matters little whether that power is called the Father in heaven or the law of Nature. Jesus taught that man should be concerned first of all about righteousness and justice among men. Other matters will take care of themselves.

Nature is not affected by color, race, circumstance, politics or religious belief. Men all over the world have different religions and political orientations. Yet the same snow that blankets Chicago covers the rest of the world. Check your history books closely and you will discover that the intervention of Nature really defeated Hitler's army. Hitler was on his way to Moscow and twenty-six straight days of snow halted his tanks. Nature will intervene to protect her underdogs and to resist unnatural oppression. When man dares to violate the nature of man, Nature herself will produce the necessary reaction.

A Callus on His Soul

If a man puts a tight shoe on his foot, so that the shoe continually rubs against the foot, he will get a corn. If he wears the tight shoe long enough, the corn will turn into a callus. Man does not want to have a corn or a callus on his foot, but Nature says that nothing shall rub against her own. If a man still persists in wearing the tight shoe, the callus will swell, getting harder and tougher, and eventually the shoe will wear out. I have never seen the shoe which would be able to wear out one of Nature's feet.

America has put a tight shoe on the Negro and now he has a callus on his soul. The Negro wants and needs a new shoe. America owes him that, because she took the Negro barefoot from Africa and put the shoe on him that was manacled to the plow which planted her cotton and to the ties that built her railroads. The greatness of America was built on the back of the Negro whose shoes still do not fit well enough to enable him to walk like a man.

Suddenly America seems to be willing to give the Negro a new pair of shoes. But she has disregarded the callus on his soul. Suppose a man wears a size 8 shoe, but all of his life he has been pushed into a size 7½. It is not enough to say you are going to give this man a brand-new size 8 shoe. Rather, you have to give him a size 9 or 10 and work on his corns and bunions until he is ready once again to wear the size 8. The Negro in America needs more than a new shoe. He needs a special shoe and the care of a doctor. The Negro needs special treatment.

When America decided that she must solve the missile gap, she did not entrust the solution of the problem to

Senators and Congressmen who had never had a course in nuclear physics. Rather America went all over the world and assembled the best minds money could buy. Only highly trained and specialized scientists could solve the missile gap. America laid the problem before these brilliant minds and said honestly: "This is the problem. We don't know how to solve it. The solution is up to you."

When the ghetto becomes a laboratory instead of a battleground, the social problem in America can be solved. America must listen honestly to the cries of the ghetto and apply the best available minds to the solution of the problem. Top sociologists, psychiatrists, and social scientists are needed rather than blue ribbon panels to investigate the cause of riots. Civil disorder is Nature's violent reaction to the tight shoe system of oppression in America. And until social pediatricians do the necessary footwork, civil disorder will continue.

Nature Protects Her Own

Even in the midst of violent reaction, it is interesting to see how Nature protects her underdogs. Have you ever stopped to consider what a dangerous weapon the Molotov cocktail is? It is the most dangerous weapon in the world to the user. Consider how dangerous it is to put gasoline in a bottle, insert a rag or a piece of paper, hold it, light it, stand back and throw it. Yet you have never read about a rioter suffering third-degree burns from a Molotov cocktail. Somehow Nature protects her underdogs who are protesting the violation of the nature of man.

A newsman once asked me where Negroes learned to make Molotov cocktails. I said that I couldn't speak for all Negroes, but I learned to make a Molotov cocktail when I was five years old. The newsman was shocked and said, aghast, "Who would be so mean and low as to teach a five-year-old kid to make a Molotov cocktail?" So I told him. That white real estate broker who rented a house to my momma and her six kids with no toilet. We learned to make Molotov cocktails peeing in a milk bottle. And if you don't think that is harder than pouring gasoline into a bottle, just ask my sister.

We have all read stories of fires where a man has run into his burning house and rescued his wife, his six kids, and half of the furniture. After the ordeal is over, he cannot explain how he did it. But at the moment of crisis, Nature intervened to give him superhuman strength.

Nature is not affected by finance. If someone offered you ten thousand dollars to let them touch you on your eyeball without you blinking, you would never collect the money. At the very last moment, Nature would force you to blink your eye. Nature will protect her own.

As America has feebly attempted to solve the social problem of the black ghetto, she has disregarded the basic laws of Nature and has created the conditions of hostility and resentment which are being openly expressed through violence in the streets. If I have been hit by an automobile and I am lying in the gutter with my leg bleeding, naturally I will be grateful when someone comes along and puts a tourniquet on my leg. I am grateful because the emergency first aid is an indication that my wound will be healed and my life will be saved. But if my treatment stops with the tourniquet, I am going to die anyway.

The person who would save my life must have the will to follow the treatment all the way through. He must rush me to the hospital, after the bleeding has been stopped, so that doctors can treat my artery. Though the tourniquet stops the bleeding, if left on too long eventually it will produce gangrene in my leg and I will die. When that happens, I naturally resent the original first aid because it was a false hope. I might just as well have bled to death in the first place. The man in the ghetto naturally resents partial first aid approaches to the treatment of his problem. He wants a full-scale commitment to his problem and a thorough cure.

The shoe of oppression tightly grips the calloused soul of the Negro in America. Nature demands that the tight system must be removed. Will America pursue a course of justice and righteousness, as Jesus suggested is proper activity among men, so that the calloused soul of the black man can grow, develop, and flourish? Or will America continue to violate the nature of man, so that Nature will cause the callus to become hard and tough and swell to the proportions of breaking through the system and destroying the shoe? Only America can answer. But the immediate proclamation of the black ghetto is clear: the shoe's too tight.

IX

For this reason I bow my knees before the Father, from whom every family in heaven and on earth is named.

EPHESIANS 3:14–15

THE NAME GAME

There seems to be an unconscious, unwritten tradition in America today that a first name indicates ownership. A tavern, restaurant or nightclub owner attaches his name to his property to clearly establish who is the controlling party in determining the policies of the establishment; Joe's Place, Frank's Restaurant or Art D'Lugoff's Village Gate. The first name, the name preceding the property, indicates ownership.

The same tradition applies to the many ethnic groups which comprise the total population of America—the Irish, Italians, Spanish, Chinese, and so on. Traditional terminology refers to these ethnic groups as Irish-Americans, Italian-Americans, Spanish-Americans or Chinese-Americans. The unwritten assumption is that the Irish, Italians, Spanish or Chinese are part owners of America. America belongs to them, rather than their belonging to America. They each have a role to play in determining the controlling policies of the American establishment.

There are two glaring exceptions to this unwritten tradition—the American-Indian and the American-Negro. The original owners of America's soil are never referred to as Indian-Americans. Nor are the emancipated slaves designated as Negro-Americans. And certainly it cannot be said that the term Afro-American has been generally accepted by white America.

Since the first name indicates ownership, the terms American-Indian or American-Negro mean that America owns the Indian and the Negro. Indians and Negroes stand apart from other ethnic groups in the eyes of America in being denied their proper role as part owners of this nation. Traditional terminology is a daily reminder that America stole her land from its native inhabitants and kidnaped me to cultivate that land.

The scripture verse from the letter to the Ephesians indicates that all men are justly named by an authority beyond governmental policies and social patterns of behavior. Men are owned or controlled by right or by wrong. And they are properly named by their allegiance to right or wrong. The only meaningful category is Right Americans and Wrong Americans. The time is long overdue to begin to call each American, and America herself, by the proper name.

The Fish-In

All my life I have had a passionate sympathy for the Indian in America; because I knew that Wrong America slanted her history books. When the Indians won a battle, the history books called it a "massacre." When the cavalry won a battle, on the other hand, it was called "a great victory." The Indians' real problems have never been given a fair hearing. One day, while I was playing a nightclub date in Seattle, Washington, I finally had the opportunity to see and hear the Indians' problems firsthand and to join with them in their struggle against injustice.

I received an invitation from Janet and Donald McCloud, Pauline Matheson and William Frank to attend a powwow sponsored by an organization called the Survival of the American Indians. The organization was formed as a response to existing governmental policy to help the Indian and protect him. Whenever there is a complaint to the government concerning Indian problems, it is sent to the Bureau of Indian Affairs. From what I have seen, this is about equal to the Ku Klux Klan running the enforcement arm of civil rights legislation.

I went to the powwow to ask what I could do to help. After talking about some of the Indian problems in the state of Washington, we developed the idea of a "fish-in." The basic injustice we sought to correct was this. The Nisqually Indians have had a treaty with the government for 112 years which gives them the right to fish in any water, using any means.

The state of Washington decided it is bigger than the treaty. But it is unfair to point a finger at the state of Washington without also putting the blame on Washington, D.C. America has gone all over the world dropping bombs and upholding treaties. We are in Vietnam today and we are one of the few countries that did not sign the treaty. Now we turn our backs on the Indian in America, who is the oldest resident American, and say, "*Your* treaty was no good."

The state of Washington has three types of fishermen: the commercial fisherman, the sports fisherman, and the Indian. Of these three, the sports fisherman is the most important from the state's point of view. The fish involved in our dispute, steelhead, is one of the most difficult fish to catch. Sportsmen spend a great deal of money trying to catch it, which helps the economy (not of the fish, but of the state). Only the sports and commercial fishermen are given any real consideration by the state. In addition, Russian and Japanese fishermen fish in the international waters three miles offshore. There is continual furor over the activities of these foreign fishermen, but nothing has been done. So out of all the steelheads being caught in the whole state of Washington, Indians catch less than 2 percent.

Why? The state of Washington tells the Indian he cannot fish with a net. He must use a fishhook. But such a ruling does not take into consideration the peculiar nature of the fish. Wherever a fish is born, it will return to that same area at spawning time. Even though the fish has been halfway around the world, it will buck the stream and come back home to lay its eggs and die. At this time, the fish doesn't have an appetite. If the Indian is forced to fish with a hook, obviously the steelhead is not going to eat it.

So it is like a game the state of Washington is playing with the Indian. It is the same as the South's attitude about voting rights. The South has always said, "We don't mind Negroes voting, we just don't want them coming in crowds." Yet the Negro knows he will be beaten and lynched if he comes to the polls by himself. The state of Washington said, "We don't mind the Indian fishing, but he must use a hook." When the Indians started fishing with nets, the state brought out an injunction against them.

Justice or "Just Us"?

After experiencing such unfair legal maneuvers, you can imagine the image the Indian has of the courthouse. An Indian woman said to me, "You might say that the courthouse represents justice, but what that word means to the Indian is 'just us.'" When you see firsthand the many injustices against the Indian, you begin to realize what "just us" means. An Indian will be arrested and claim his treaty rights. The court will insist that he prove he is an Indian. I couldn't prove legally that I am a Negro. The Indian is forced to spend a fortune, using up all of his legal funds, proving to the court that he is an Indian.

We must realize that America *was* the Indian's country. Either America should admit that the Indian is an American and say she is sorry for what she has done—this would involve reviewing existing treaties and, wherever they have been violated, paying reparation—or America should say openly that the Indian is not an American. Then it becomes the Indian's duty to throw off colonialism, as people all over the world are doing. They are reclaiming their land, which is the Indian's only alternative, if America is not going to share equally with him and admit that he is a part owner of this country.

The Indian is a partial owner of America as is every other minority group in this country. Every minority has had a struggle to realize this ownership. It has always bothered me to hear people pride themselves on their victory against a nation full of bigotry. People say the Irish had a fight and won. So did the Jews, the Catholics, the Italians, and other minorities. But it is a pity that the Irish, Jews, Italians, and others did not fight for the Constitution instead of themselves. We will probably look back one day and be forced to say the same thing about Negroes. Somebody has to fight for the Constitution and do away with all bigotry once and for all.

If we continue to make the mistake of turning our backs, we will find one day that the biggest problem in America's history is the Indian. The only way for the Indian to be recognized as an American is for America to lose a war with Russia or China. The conqueror, in taking over the country, would recognize the Indian as an American and give him the same kind of dirty treatment other Americans would receive. This should make a nation full of savages ashamed, but America sleeps with this truth every night.

The issues involved in the injustice to the Indian must be heard and dealt with before it is too late. If the Communists were up on the reservations organizing the Indians, or if the Indians were armed and shooting people on the highways, the whole country would be immediately concerned. We only seem to get concerned about a problem when the Communists are concerned. If we had been concerned about Vietnam before the Communists, we might not have lost one American life. We never seem to be able to handle an issue in this country *before* it becomes an open problem. I hope this will not be the same pattern with the Indian problem.

Red Power

There are some encouraging rays of light in the dark night of America's injustice to the Indian. The Indian is voting now for the first time in many parts of the country, as a result of the deaths in Alabama and the voting rights legislation. There have been laws giving the Indian the right to vote, but the literacy tests have always stood in his way. There are thousands of Indians who speak only their tribal tongue. With the lifting of the requirement regarding the English language, these Indians can now vote.

In the little town of St. John's, Arizona, Indians marched for voter registration. There are ten thousand Indians in that area. The reaction was the same as we saw in Mississippi. People said, "These Indians are not responsible; they don't know what the politicians are talking about. They don't even understand the English language." That only means the politicians are not responsible. If the Indian is ignorant of the language—due to America's failure to educate him—he should not have to suffer the penalty of not voting. If anyone should suffer it should be the politician. He must learn the Indian's language to discuss political issues, if he wants the Indian vote. Otherwise, the Indian has every right to vote him out of office.

Our "fish-in" demonstration produced encouraging reactions. By publicizing this particular issue of treaty violation, we were able to begin to open the eyes of America to her tragic disregard of the Indian. When my wife and I were placed in jail for fishing, there was world-wide reaction. I received telegrams from Bertrand Russell, Dr. Martin Luther King, James Farmer, and the unions representing teachers and college professors.

When we first started demonstrating, the reaction within the state of Washington was mixed. But in a short period of time, college students in the state began holding demonstrations on behalf of the Indian. Radio and television talk shows began to take a good look at the problem. People began to see that the Indian has a just demand. They saw the issue in concrete terms which they could easily understand. They knew there was a fish involved and a very powerful fish economically. Such a personal reaction was something totally new for the state of Washington and a beginning of an honest confrontation with the Indian problem.

An aroused citizenry should now take the problem of the Indian directly to the White House. A group of Indians should hold a vigil on the White House lawn until LBJ decides that Indians count too. The Justice Department should be made to protect the Indian treaties. Such a vigil would let the whole world see that, if America will break her treaty with the Indian, she might not uphold her treaty with anyone.

I do not believe this about America. I think Americans would die defending their treaties. The day must come when America shows the same concern for her treaties with the Indians as she does for treaties with other countries. Other Indian treaties are being broken; treaties concerning timber rights, for example. We may be having some

"Timber Wiggles" in the future. This will be the maximum expression of nonviolent demonstration. The demonstrator will climb a tree and when he hears "Timber!" he will ride down with it nonviolently.

The day these problems with the Indian are solved will be the day America can breathe her first clean breath of fresh air. Moral pollution is more destructive than air pollution. But if we clean up every other problem and leave the Indian in his misery, the shadow of shame will destroy us.

Black Power

America today is so obsessed by color. We have a habit in America of labeling with a color that which we fear or do not understand. When I look at a map of the world, I see a country named China. Yet America constantly refers to that country as Red China. Our fear of Communism causes us to attach the color label. The label symbolizes our fear and resentment.

The Muslims in America practice a religion which is deeply rooted in world history and shared by many people the world over. Yet because of America's fear and lack of understanding, the religion is labeled in this country Black Muslim. A couple of years ago, a newsman asked me, "Were you surprised when Cassius Clay announced he was a Black Muslim?" I told him, "I was surprised when he announced he was a Muslim. I knew about the rest of it."

Yet, in spite of America's color obsession, she claims not to be able to understand the slogan "Black Power." I refuse to believe that the country which has been to the moon and sent back pictures cannot understand two simple words. Black—both Negroes and whites know what that is. And power—certainly white folks should know what it is. White folks pretend not to know what black power means and Negroes lie about not understanding it. They do not want white folks to know they understand perfectly.

When newsmen ask me what Black Power means, I tell them Negroes have always had black power. Joe Louis had the fastest left hand in the history of boxing. That is black power. Jackie Robinson's lifetime batting average is well over 300. That is black power. And if my wife got a divorce from me today, the judge would give her everything. That is certainly black power.

America knows the meaning of black power and that is why those two words frighten so many people. I got on a bus the other day in Chicago and I was tired. The bus was crowded and I didn't see an empty seat. So I paid my fare, stood at the front of the bus and yelled, "Black Power!" Two little old ladies got up and gave me their seat. And they were colored!

The fear of black power is not based on an ignorance of the meaning of the words, but on a failure to understand how black power came into being. White America created black power. For every one Negro in America there are ten white folks. If America was truly a land of equal opportunity, so that neighborhoods were integrated with whites and blacks living side by side, every Negro would have ten white neighbors. We would be so meek and humble we would beg to join the Ku Klux Klan.

But instead, Negroes are concentrated in small pockets of the urban areas of this nation. A public housing project is constructed and a hundred and some odd thousand people are crowded into a six-block area—all black. This concentration and density of population are the ingredients of black power.

I know that there are more human beings on the face of the earth than there are vicious beasts. When I walk down the street in Chicago or New York City, I am not worried about being bitten by a tiger, stomped by an elephant or seized by a gorilla. But when I take my kids to the zoo, I have the sneaking suspicion that if I am ever going to be attacked by a beast, it will happen there. All of the vicious beasts are concentrated in the zoo. This gathering of animals potentially represents animal power.

If I walk down Michigan Avenue in Chicago, I do not worry about being drowned. But if I saw someone pour a hundred thousand gallons of water into the street, I would be worried. Because right across the street is water power—Lake Michigan. The man who burns only candles and kerosene lamps in his house is not worried about being the victim of electric power. Only when he comes into contact with electric current, when he changes a fuse or fixes a socket, does a man stand a chance of being electrocuted.

Not until you understand how black power came into being can you give a sensible meaning to the familiar words. When white America fully understands how it has created black power, it can begin to predict the results of the power it has unleashed. But to pretend not to understand the words is foolish.

The creator should understand what he has created. Parents do not go to the baby nine months after that night of sex and ask, "Where did you come from?" Rather the baby comes to the parents early in life and asks, "How did I get here?" We all know the silly, stupid answers parents usually give to the baby's question. They are as foolish as the definitions people give for the two words black power.

If anyone should ask about the meaning of black power, it should be Negroes. Negroes did not create black power. All at once we looked up one day, from deep within the ghettoized existence into which white America had compressed us, and said, "Black Power." Now that the

Negro realizes he has black power, the questioning title of Martin Luther King's book is a sobering thought for the entire nation, "Where do we go from here?"

Spontaneous Combustion

Webster's Dictionary gives many definitions for both the words "black" and "power." When these definitions are set in the context of the ghetto conditions which white America has forced upon the Negro, the results of black power are easy to understand. Black is defined at one point as "soiled with dirt," "opposite of white," and "hostile." Power is defined as "exerted energy," "force," or "might." I am immediately reminded of the natural phenomenon of spontaneous combustion.

Take some dirty, greasy, oily, black rags and throw them in a closet. Then close the closet door and shut it tight so that no air can circulate. It makes no difference whether the closet is in the rich man's mansion or the ghetto apartment. After a period of time, Nature will produce a reaction. The rags will burst into flame and burn down the house. You can stand outside the door and curse the rags; call them "black, dirty, greasy things," but Nature will not listen. Cursing will not help at all. The only way to prevent the destructive fire is to open the closet door so that air can circulate.

The poor inhabitants of the tightly closeted ghettos of America are this nation's black, oily, greasy rags. America has kept the door to opportunity tightly closed. No air circulates in the ghetto. In the summer, the ghetto streets are cooler than the apartments. Ghetto inhabitants are choking from the lack of air—from unemployment, welfare injustices, inferior education, and the degradation of poverty. The door of the ghetto is so tightly shut that even the rats cannot escape! Is it any wonder that the closeted ghettos burst into flame? The flaming response in the streets of ghettos across this nation is a natural reaction—spontaneous combustion.

And still the government prefers to curse the rags rather than open the door. Anti-riot legislation comes quicker than federal money for equal opportunity.

The Hungry Mind

Black is elsewhere defined as "sold or distributed in violation of official priorities; as in black market." The history of being black in America is one of Negroes being sold and distributed in violation of official priorities. The black man began his history in America by being sold into slavery. He has since been distributed into the ghetto slums of the North and the broken-down shacks of the South. Power is defined as "a faculty, as of thinking or hearing." This concentration of black power which white America has created, sold, and distributed is now beginning to use these important faculties.

Go into the black ghetto and you will notice a change over the past few years. Twenty or thirty years ago, the ghetto dweller had an empty stomach. This is not true any more. I know people on relief who drink Diet-Rite; or the ghetto equivalent Low Calorie Liz. I remember when I was a kid in the ghetto, a turnip was a delicacy. Today, some of the poorest people in the country are on diets. In my ghetto neighborhood, the fat kid in the block was a freak.

Today the man in the ghetto has a full stomach and a hungry mind. There is a big difference. The hungry mind will not tolerate the same things the empty stomach did. The empty stomach is affected by smell. The hungry mind, is affected by sound. And things do not sound right to this hungry ghetto mind. It does not sound right to that black ghetto mother to tell her you cannot get the rat out of her baby's crib, but you can send pictures back from Mars. Nor does it sound right to tell her she is making progress; when the same rat which was biting her children ten years ago is still biting her new baby today. Her hungry mind tells her the truth. In her own instinctive, uneducated way that ghetto mother knows that, if Russia announced it was going to rid the country of rats in five years to prove the superiority of Communism, America would eradicate rats in six months. If scientists said that after ten years of research, they have found that the inside of a rat's belly is lined with uranium, a federal law would be passed, with stiff penalties imposed, making it a federal crime *not* to report rats to the proper authorities. In five years' time, ghetto parents would be taking their kids to the zoo to show them what rats used to look like.

The hungry mind in the ghetto is sensitive to the violation of official priority. The federal government announced it was going to declare war on poverty. The hungry mind of the man in the ghetto knew what the words "declare war" *should* mean. The ghetto brother has had to fight all of America's wars. The man in the ghetto knows that the white man in this country means business when he says he is going to declare war. So when he heard those familiar, vicious words, "Declare War," the man in the ghetto expected to get out of poverty overnight.

But the federal government did not mean "Declare War." It appropriated just enough money to tease poverty not conquer it. If the government had said in the first place that it intended to tease poverty, the hungry mind of the man in the ghetto would have understood. He has been teased and taunted by poverty all of his life. The government made its fatal mistake by trying to pull a fraud and a trick on the ghetto.

The poor man in the ghetto is the one person you cannot trick. His hungry mind is too naturally brilliant. He will not fall for any trick and he will see through any fraud. Nor can you steal from the man in the ghetto, as many politicians have tried to do with anti-poverty funds. It is possible to steal a billion dollars from the missile program, or any government contract, but you cannot steal from the poor man in the ghetto.

At one time I had forty pairs of shoes in my house. If someone walked in and stole five pairs, I probably would never have missed the shoes if I did not actually see the theft. But if someone steals the left shoe of the poor man in the ghetto, he misses it immediately. He cannot go to work because someone messed up his only pair of shoes. When I was a poor kid in the ghetto, a rat came into the bedroom and ran off with my sock. I missed it immediately. I couldn't go to school that morning. It was too cold to go outside without any socks on at all. And I would look like a fool wearing just one sock. So chemistry class had to wait. The rat messed up my whole day.

It is interesting to note the striking similarity between the concentrated mass of black power at the bottom of the system of oppression in this country and the small group of wealthy elite at the top of that system. As it is useless for the mugger to hold up the very poor man in the ghetto, so also is it futile to mug the very rich man on Sutton Place. Neither man will be carrying any money. The very poor man has no money, period. And the very rich man carries only credit cards. The rich man travels all over the world with no more than fifty dollars in his pocket. The poor man goes where he wants to go with his pockets empty. The difference is the distance traveled.

Both the rich man and the poor man in the ghetto have two operating addresses. The rich man has his private, protected home address, which he is very discreet about revealing. And he also has his downtown office address where he conducts his business during certain hours. If you try to make an appointment to meet the poor man in the ghetto, the chances are he will give you two addresses. He will give you the address of his home or the place he is staying. And he will give you his "business" address—his special street corner. "Meet me on Sixty-third and Cottage Grove after ten o'clock and we'll take care of business," he will say.

Neither the very rich man nor the very poor man allow themselves to be worried about society. The rich man is in control of society so he doesn't have to worry. The poor man has no place in society so he doesn't give a damn about it. The rich man rejects society because he just doesn't have to be concerned about it. The poor man rejects society because it is the oppressive force which contains him in his poverty.

The numbers involved in this social rejection are the crucial factor. Some thirty families comprise the very wealthy elite. But there are millions of poor ghetto residents who comprise the concentration of black power. When the contagion of social rejection spreads through the millions of black masses reaching epidemic proportions, the rich man's money will not save him from infection.

Channeling the Flood

The decisive and crucial definition of black is "one of a dark-skinned race, a Negro or one having some Negro blood." And the equally decisive definition of power is "authority or right; an authority vested in one person to dispose of, or create rights in, the property of another." Black power is a moral reminder to Wrong America. It is a slogan of right issuing from the poverty and injustice of the ghetto of the North and the squalor and starvation of the deprivation of the South. Black power is poor power or right power reminding this nation that all who live under the Constitution are part owners of America. All Americans have a right to a decent wage, to own their own businesses, to own their own property and to choose and elect their own public officials who will serve as their power of attorney at the seat of government. The concentrated weight of black power which white America has created will either balance the scales of justice or destroy the system of checks and balances so that a new standard of measure can be created. Whichever alternative is the final result, black power has the moral authority of right and the blessing of the Declaration of Independence.

Walking into the ghetto today is like standing in a valley and looking up at the snowcap on a mountain. The wise man knows that in the spring of the year the snow will thaw and great floods will pour down the mountain sweeping everything in the valley away. There are many reactions the residents of the valley can have in the face of this potential disaster, both wise and foolish.

The valley dwellers may look up and curse and resent the snowcap; which makes as much sense as passing anti-riot legislation in response to the problems of the ghetto. Or the valley dwellers may build a dam and try to contain the potential flood. But no dam made by the hands of man will be finally able to withstand the flood, which is Nature's reaction to man's mistreatment of the land, of the trees, and of the river. Nor will the National Guard or federal troops ultimately be able to withstand the natural reaction of man's inhumanity to his fellow man.

The wise inhabitants of the valley will have the foresight to redirect this potential flood, this great power of light, energy, and destruction, into something constructive, such as channeling the flood into hydroelectric power or irrigation systems. The potential curse becomes a blessing when the proper foresight, wisdom, and understanding are applied. The concentrated force and energy of black power could be America's richest blessing and most important natural resource if channeled into constructive expressions. America's challenge is to recognize the power of right and the capacity of black and to combine them both.

X

Broken down is the city of chaos;
Every house is shut up, so that
    no one can enter;
In the streets there is an outcry
    for wine.
All joy has reached its eventide,
The mirth of the world is gone;
Desolation is left in the city,
And its gates are battered to ruins.

ISAIAH 24:10–12

THE CITY OF CHAOS

From his description of urban life, it is hard to believe that the prophet Isaiah had never visited the United States. His words sound like an eyewitness report from the riot-torn streets of Newark, Watts, Harlem or Detroit. The prophet seems to be sensitive to the problems which currently plague our cities. The failure of urban renewal programs has produced "broken-down cities of chaos." The tragic pattern of segregated housing demonstrates to Negroes at least that "every house is shut up, so that no one can enter." And anyone who has walked the streets of the black ghetto on Saturday night has heard the "outcry for wine."

But the prophetic word which hits closest to home for me personally is the proclamation, "The mirth of the world is gone." The prophet seems to be saying that there is nothing humorous about the city of chaos. I would agree. Though they mean to be paying me a compliment, I am tired of people crediting me with helping to solve the racial problem in this country through humor.

The truth is that I have the ability to amuse many people and humor pays my rent. But never be under the illusion that humor will solve any social problems. The world did not laugh Hitler out of existence. Some day a cure for cancer will be discovered. Believe me, it will not be discovered through humor. The cure for cancer will come as a result of dedicated research by the best medical minds available; men who are willing to face the problem honestly and devote all of their energies to developing a cure.

People also talk about my sacrificing so much for my people. It is true that I have lost hundreds of thousands of dollars in the struggle for human dignity; through travel expenses, legal fees, and canceled engagements. But, to be honest, it was not a personal sacrifice. I am more selfish than that. When the white wino in this country has more rights than the black millionaire, it is the rich man who is in trouble. I am just trying to free my blackness before I free my bank account.

It is interesting how much the prophet Isaiah's description of the city of chaos, a city which ends up in desolation with its gates battered to ruins, reminds us of the familiar pressure points in modern urban America. "Every house is shut up, so that no one can enter." The open occupancy marches in Chicago, led by Dr. Martin Luther King, revealed a condition which could create one of the biggest blood baths this country has ever known. And it is a condition which exists only in the North.

The Difference Between the South and North

As you watched the television reports of demonstrations in the South, you saw southern cops misusing civil rights demonstrators with cattle prods, clubs, tear gas, dogs, horses, and boots. But you did not see the demonstrators being attacked by large white mobs. The reason is that the southern cop is a different creature than his northern counterpart. He has a different image. Why? Because he is not out on the street corner shaking people down, dealing in dope and prostitution. The southern cop means business and will misuse both white and Negro who get in his way. When a cop in Birmingham tells white folks to get off the street corner, they run! But when a cop up North tells people to move on, they will turn on him and start fighting. Such is the disrespect and resentment for the cop in the North. When the civil rights demonstrators left the all-white neighborhoods in Chicago, where open occupancy marches were taking place, fighting continued with the cops. Many whites were arrested after the marchers had left the area. Whites resented the presence of marchers in "their" neighborhood and resented equally the cops who were protecting the marchers. The resentment burst forth in open attack of both cops and Negroes.

So in the South, civil rights demonstrators were attacked, by and large, by the cops and not by large white mobs. The difference between being attacked by the cop and being attacked by the mob is that the cop will not stab you, nor will he throw bricks and bottles. I would personally rather swallow tear gas than be stabbed.

The door to desolation and chaos in the city is opened in the North when someone in a white mob shoots and hits a Negro cop. And the cop retaliates by shooting five times and killing five whites. If this happens, you have a blood bath on your hands. Watch these northern demonstrations and see the police brutality on white folks' heads, though people seldom speak of it. We are seeing more and more that the police represent a monster which will turn on whites as well as blacks when the conditions are right. And conditions are right in the North.

You must appreciate a few things about the South to understand the difference in reaction. Every white man in the South has had a Negro working in his home. The southern white man who was only making five dollars a day could get my grandma to work for him for a quarter a day. But this white man standing in a mob surrounding a march into a northern white neighborhood has never been able to afford the luxury of a Negro in his home. Even a Negro appearing in his neighborhood is a strange thing. It is not to his southern white brother. So strange was the appearance of a Negro teen-ager in Cicero, Illinois, that he was attacked and killed by white youths. And the black youth was only in town to try to get a job.

The southern white man is familiar with Negroes. Regardless of how bigoted he is, the southern white man knows a Negro schoolteacher, a Negro doctor or a Negro minister. In the North it is easier to live an all-white existence and *never* personally know a Negro teacher, doctor or minister. When we marched for our rights in the South, the old Negro "Uncle Toms" would be sitting on the courthouse lawn, while the sheriff was across the street whipping our heads. But up North, if a Negro happened to be standing on the street corner in an all-white neighborhood during a demonstration and slip and say, "Man, those colored folks is right," he would be killed immediately. The system has been more vicious in the North than it has in the South, because it has kept Negroes and whites more distant.

Distance is a great barrier to understanding. In the North, there is a familiar pattern of segregation in housing, all-white and all-black communities. In the South, the sharecropper is underpaid and mistreated by his white employer, but he is not distant from him. The sharecropper and his family live in a shack close behind the plantation owner's mansion. If the sharecropper's baby cries in the middle of the night, his employer will hear the cry in the big house. There is a proximity of living and understanding. When I was seventeen years old, my ghetto home was so far from my employer's neighborhood that I could tell him anything about myself and he would believe it. I could tell him I was twenty-four, married with three children. When I wanted to take a week off, I would call in and tell the boss one of my babies was sick.

The Right to Walk Down a Street

This distance has produced the situation in which "all joy has reached its eventide" in the northern cities of chaos. The extent of joyless and dangerous hypocrisy is becoming more and more evident in the North. Again, the marches into all-white neighborhoods have served to bring this pitiful hypocrisy to the surface. Martin Luther King announced that he is going to march on a northern real estate office and his march is blocked on the street corner before he reaches his destination. When that happens, the street corner becomes the immediate business of the day. And the demonstrators ought to stay on that corner for as many hours as it takes to obtain a guarantee of free and safe passage. A new issue is created; that of the right to walk down an American street. And that issue is not solved by sitting at the bargaining table with businessmen, clergymen, and realtors. It is solved by forcing a resolution of the problem at the time and place of confrontation. If I am going fishing for salmon and twelve whales are standing in the way, I have to deal immediately with the whales before I can get what I am really after.

I think the right to walk down an American street is equally if not more important than the right to own a home. Yet, if Martin Luther King says he is going to march in a northern white neighborhood for eighteen straight hours to demonstrate for the right of open occupancy, everyone gets upset. Court injunctions are served against him to prohibit marching. But the same people who are upset about that march in the northern white neighborhood can justify Martin Luther King going down to Mississippi during the James Meredith March and walking 250 miles to rid southern Negroes of fear. There is no difference between a Negro being afraid to walk the highways of Mississippi and a Negro being afraid to walk the streets of Cicero, Illinois.

This is a basic problem in northern cities. Many neighborhoods are "shut up, so that no one can enter." White folks are afraid to walk through colored neighborhoods and colored folks are afraid to walk through white neighborhoods. With a little imagination and understanding, that problem could be solved immediately.

Negro plain-clothes cops should be sent into white neighborhoods. Dress them up to look like ordinary John Doe Negroes. The first time white folks on the street corner start to clown with those cops in disguise, arrest them and lock them up. White plain-clothes cops should be sent into colored neighborhoods. Dress them up to look like Joe Square Ofay white cat. And when my racist black brother starts to clown with one of the masquerading white cops, lock him up too. In six months the problem of fear of walking in certain neighborhoods would be solved. Not because an atmosphere of love would have been created, but simply because a person doesn't know who it is safe to hit.

Martin Luther King told the truth about this crisis of distance and understanding during one of the Chicago marches. He said, "I see more hate here than I did in the South." I was surprised to hear Dr. King say that. Because I thought he knew it all along. I thought Dr. King hit the South first because he knew he could overcome it quicker. The crucial difference between the North and the South is this: *in the South the white man has misused Negroes physically, but in the North he has misused us mentally.*

Dreaming in a Movie

The kid in the northern ghetto learns of this mental abuse very early in life. I remember in 1942, when I was ten years old, I stole enough milk bottles to go to a movie. I cashed in the bottles and paid ten cents admission and had enough left over for a penny's worth of jelly beans. My friend and I sat in the front row of the Circle Theatre in St. Louis and watched *The Barefoot Contessa* starring Humphrey Bogart and Ava Gardner. And after fifteen minutes, I got up and left the theater. The mental abuse was more than I could endure. My friend couldn't understand why I left.

I was going to the movies back in 1942 for the same reason as the rest of America—to dream. The theater itself was a dream world with its big chandeliers and ornaments. But even at the age of ten, I realized that the American Dream was not for me. I knew that if I had cashed in enough bottles to take my sister to that movie, she couldn't have fallen in love with Humphrey Bogart, any more than I could fall in love with Ava Gardner. I was too young to know anything about sex, but the false dream was still painfully obvious. The only person on the movie screen for me to fall in love with was Beulah and that would be like falling in love with my own momma.

Going to the movie in a Negro neighborhood is an experience which shows firsthand the reaction to mental abuse. The audience is loud, unruly, laughing in the wrong places and pulling for the Indians against the cowboys.

The movie theater is the only place the ghetto brother has ever had the American white man to himself for a little while without the cop looking down his back. The noise, the hooting, and the laughing in the wrong place is a protest against mental abuse.

I remember coming home from the movie theater one day in tears. I had just seen *Frankenstein*. My momma asked me what was wrong. Still crying, I told momma, "I just saw *Frankenstein* and the monster didn't scare me." Momma couldn't explain it and I couldn't understand it. I was afraid I wasn't normal. But now that I look back, I realize why I wasn't frightened. Somehow I unconsciously realized that the Frankenstein monster was chasing what was chasing me. Here was a monster, created by a white man, turning upon his creator. The horror movie was merely a parable of life in the ghetto. The monstrous life of the ghetto has been created by the white man. Only now in the city of chaos are we seeing the monster created by oppression turn upon its creator. As a ten-year-old kid, when I saw this parable enacted on the movie screen, this vicious, mentally abusive system caused me to pull for the monster!

It was the same when I went to see *King Kong*. When he was on the Empire State Building grabbing for that airplane, I was pulling for King Kong. If there had been one Negro on that plane, I would have had a different reaction. What kind of mental abuse is it which teaches a kid to identify with a gorilla?

In College Under False Pretenses

Even education itself can be used as the agent of mental abuse. I had been taught at home that if I got the proper education, white folks would respect me. I believed this until I was almost through college. During the midterm of my final year, a fellow Negro student came to me and told me he had failed his French exam. It dawned on me that I was in college under false pretenses. I had always assumed that a college education would gain me respect. When my friend failed French, I learned a valuable lesson.

I suddenly realized that dogs in France understand French. Dogs in Russia understand Russian. Chinese seems like a difficult language to me, but dogs in China easily understand it. I learned that man is born with all the wisdom needed to gain dignity and respect. If you have to depend upon education to gain respect, something is radically wrong. The really important lesson to learn in life is that it is the man who should be respected, not his education. A man has gained nothing in life if his education is respected and his manhood is not.

Just stop to think how many people the world over would have died if there were no such thing as blood plasma. The research and education of an American Negro, Dr. Charles Drew, made blood plasma possible. His brilliant mind used his education for the benefit of the entire human family. And yet Charles Drew bled to death in the waiting room of a Georgia hospital, following an automobile accident, because that hospital did not accept "niggers." Dr. Drew made blood plasma possible for mankind and died from the lack of it—because his skin was black. Human dignity and respect are not based on education.

The words of Isaiah, "Broken down is the city of chaos," remind us of the two kinds of urban renewal in America today. There is planned urban renewal which uses tractors and bulldozers. And there is honest urban renewal which uses brick. History provides striking parallels. We have all heard of the burning of Rome, but we fail to relate it to what is happening in America today. In the days of the Roman Empire, there was no tractors or bulldozers. Urban renewal could only come about by burning down the city and starting again. When government-planned urban renewal fails today, the result is "Burn, baby, burn," which is simply urban renewal without grass, drawing boards or city planners. Honest urban renewal comes when ghetto residents take things into their own hands and dramatically say, "We will not be forced to live in ghetto conditions any longer." When government-planned urban renewal fails to remove the blight of the ghetto, honest urban renewal is the only alternative. The gate of the city is battered to ruins and desolation rules the city of chaos.

"Please, Sir, Get Off My Back"

The city of chaos dramatically represents the plight of the Negro in America today. It is like a man jumping on your back and getting a free ride. After two weeks of carrying your unwelcome burden, you look up at him and say, as meekly and humbly, as you can, "Sir, will you please get off my back?" Perhaps your rider answers, "I know I am wrong, and I sure would like to get off. But you can't expect me to jump off your back all at once. It takes time. I can tell you one thing, however. I will not ride your kids' backs." How would you react to that!

America has been riding the backs of Negroes for three hundred years. It has been a free ride. Many times the Negro has tried to tell America to get off. He didn't say it openly as did Abraham Lincoln. The Negro sang his problem to America. Listen to the words of those vicious slave songs. The blues were death songs. But the country would not listen and stayed on the Negro's back. America had too much malice to really listen. Instead, America said, "Those Negroes certainly do have rhythm. Listen to them sing."

And the Negro tried to tell America nonviolently. The Negro had to be nonviolent. How can you hit a man who is riding your back? Every time you turn around to hit him, your rider automatically turns around too! Still America said, "I can't get off just yet. You aren't quite ready for me to get off. But I promise not to ride your kids' backs."

Five years ago, when he began to seriously ask America to get off his back, the Negro changed his position slightly. All the time he has been giving America a free ride, the Negro has had his hands in his pockets. Now he has taken his hands out of his pockets and wrapped his arms around his rider's legs. What used to be a free ride for America has now become a trip.

If I wrap my arms around the legs of a man who is riding my back, my rider cannot get off even if he wants to. Now I am taking him on a trip. On my way I am remembering the words of Patrick Henry, "Give me liberty or give me death." Patrick Henry was talking about killing. I am not talking about killing anyone. I have merely decided that if liberty is worth living for, it is also worth dying for. I lived for liberty, I struggled for it. But America stayed on my back and refused to give me liberty. So I am walking down to the river to jump in. And when I jump in, the rider on my back goes with me, because my hands are still wrapped around his legs. I am not going to kill him. I am merely taking my rider under with me. Because he has refused to get off, when I commit suicide, my rider murders himself.

When he finally sees where I am going, my rider will try to make a deal. But I won't go for that. I know what he has done in the past. He wouldn't get off when I asked him. If I let my rider off on the bridge, he will still be behind me; he can still push me in the river and get away. So my rider and I must both go down together.

When the decision has been made to die rather than live under continued oppression, a shadow of death is cast from one end of the country to the other. The Psalmist said, "Though I walk through the valley of the shadow of death, I will fear no evil." The Negro in America is beyond the point of fearing evil. He has lived with it too long. He merely walks under the shadow of death in the confidence that he walks not alone. All of America rides with him.

If America does not solve her social problems in the next five years, the problems will solve America.

I want to thank and honor these "Wintertime Soldiers" who made Christmas for Mississippi possible and who continue daily to exemplify the beauty of devotion to the cause of right against the powers of wrong.

Doug Andrews
Howard Barbour
Brahim Ben Benu
Rev. James Bevel
Orzelle Billingsley
Sam and Clarence Blowe
Leonard Boudin
Rev. Malcolm Boyd
Sadie Boyd
Stanley Branche
Addie Breedlove
H. Rap Brown
Delores Cannon
Stokely Carmichael
Len Chandler
Bill Cherry
Elaine Clark
Ben Clarke
Oscar Cohen
Cubie Coleman
Berk Costello
Dr. Harvey G. Cox
Dr. Howard R. Cox
Les Crane
Daddy-O Dailey
Delores Dant
William Darden
Mary Davis
Pork Chop Davis
Sammy Davis, Jr.
Taro Delphi
Frank Ditto

Father Joseph and Phyllis Dixon
Ivanhoe Donaldson
Mike Douglas
Kathleen Dunlap
Chuck Eddy
Smiley Ellis
Mae Ethridge
James Farmer
Marty Faye
James Forman
Dr. Milton Galamison
Vince Garrity
Joe Glaser
Ralph Gleason
Barry Gray
Jack Greenberg
Garland and Emma Gregory
Pauline Gregory
Presley Gregory
Ron and Joan Gregory
Jesse Grey
Merv Griffin
Lawrence Guyot
Alice Hardiman
Edna Hargrove
Winston Hayes
Hugh Hefner
Jerry Herman
Chester Higgins
Bill Higgs
Delores and Roland Hill
Father Hogan
Lou House
Ma Houston
James Hurt
Robert Ingram
Thelma Isbell
Rev. Jesse Jackson
Rose Jennings
Bob Johnson
John L. Johnson
Killer Johnson
Myrtle Johnson
E. Rodney Jones
Father James Jones
Marv Josephson
Herbert and Gloria Jubirt
Murray Kempton
Herb Kent
Martin Luther King, Jr.
Bernie Kleinman
Paul Krassner
Marie Kriesten
Irv Kupcinet
Lawrence Landry
Anna Langford
Dr. Timothy Leary
Bernard Lee
Harold Lee
John Lewis
Bob and Marjorie Lipsyte
Sam Logan
Joan Lohman
Bob Lucas
Herb Lyon
Franklin McCarthy
Leo and Josephine McCord

Jim McGraw
Rev. James Mack
Father Mallette
Ralph Mann
James Meredith
Father Richard F. Morrisroe
Bob Moses
Elijah Muhammad
Joe Musse
Hank Oettinger
George O'Hare
Jesse Owens
Geneva Patch
Drew Pearson
Darcy Perryman
Pearl Pontillo
Tony and Lolita Porter
Adam Clayton Powell
McClellan Rector
Thomas Rector
Tommie Lee Rector
Shirley and George Rhodes
Herman Roberts
Chester Robinson
Nahaz and Mary Rogers
Steve Rose
Earless Ross
Leo Rugendorf
Jim and Jackie Sanders
Dick Shelton
Elaine Shephard
Fred Shuttlesworth
Chris and Thelma Smith
Harold Smith
Ida Smith
John Smith
Lee Smith
Martha Smith
Sadie Smith
Scott Smith
Willis Smith
Jackie Sorrell
Wesley South
Arthur Steuer
Arthur Steuer, Jr.
Jack Tanner
Studs Terkel
Cheryl Thompson
Maxine Thompson
Othello and Hortense Townsend, Jr.
Ozell and William Underwood
Rev. C. T. Vivian
Ethel Watkins
James Watkins
Mike Watley
Lynn Weeks
Tony Weitzel
Roy Wilkins
Christine Williams
Hosea Williams
Jean Williams
Jimmy Wong
Roy Woods
Rev. Andrew Young
Whitney Young